BEHIND *the* TIMES

Bachi Karkaria

Illustrations by Neelabh | *Design by* Umbrella

Foreword by Indrajit Hazra

LET TRUTH PREVAIL

First published in India, 2010
Revised edition, 2016

Times Group Books **A division of**
Bennett, Coleman & Co. Ltd.
The Times of India, 10 Daryaganj, New Delhi-110002
Phone: 011-39843333, Email: tgb@timesgroup.in

BEHIND *the* TIMES

ISBN: 978-93-80942-01-8

Price: ₹395

Printed at: Lustra Print Process Pvt. Ltd.

The Times of India has given its readers the inside story for 178 years. Nowhere's the dope on what goes on inside this amazing media machine. Is the TOI Group a terrifying god, or is it touchingly, failingly, reassuringly mortal? Does its gluttonous appetite for success play havoc with its innards? Does it have a soul, or is it quite content being a monopoly?

Mythologies can create an impenetrable aura around an organisation or they can demystify it. This small book puts itself firmly in the second camp. Ferreting out anecdotes from the lowly trenches of the Newsroom to the lofty command centres of editorial and management, it reveals power, posturing and pettiness. All with a cheeky grin.

Here you'll find the eccentricities of epic editors, the weaknesses of management strongmen, the rise and fall of shapers and fixers, the silent force of PAs, peons and other foot soldiers. You will hear the cannon boom of media wars, smell the smoke in the Giri-Nandy shootout at Bori Bunder; share the top secret mission that is the Budget edition; and catch the glint of stilettos in the Battle of the Bombay Bawis. You will be party to the strategy and skirmishes behind the amazing makeover of the dowager into a babe. And you can choose between the ghosts stalking the silenced corridors or the Phantom who sets the jungle drums a-pounding with the slightest flicker in his hooded eyes. You'll get a ringside view of good times, sad times, and changing times.

Warmly, wittily, these stories reveal the what, how and why of the TOI.

Alec Smart

Bachi Karkaria

Bachi Karkaria has lived, loved and laughed with the Times Group for almost thirty years. She learnt her craft – and her irreverence – from the legendary Khushwant Singh at the Illustrated Weekly of India *in Mumbai, imbibed a purist culture at* The Statesman *in her native Kolkata, and returned to stay at the* Times of India. *She edited the* Sunday Times, *started* Metropolis *on Saturday and* Bombay Times, *invigorated the languishing Bangalore edition of the TOI, and after a brief departure to* Mid-Day, *came back as Resident Editor, Delhi, and then National Metro Editor. She is currently a media consultant and trainer.*

Her specializations are AIDS, the urban churn and the creation of reader-centric newspapers, though she is arguably best known for her column, Erratica. She was the first Indian on the board of the Paris-based World Editors Forum, and has written several books.

Karkaria is a third-generation journalist. Her elder son, Urvaksh, continues the tradition as a business reporter in the US. The younger Rishad has followed his dad into marketing.

Foreword: Truths, Half-truths and Fiction

Birinchi Baba, that great conman in Satyajit Ray's 1964 film *Mahapurush* who poses as a guru and claims that he hung out with the Buddha and taught Einstein that E=mc2, is asked by a member of his swooning congregation, "Prabhu, did you know Jesus Christ?" Birinchi replies looking misty-eyed into the distance and says, "People say, crucifiction. I say crucifact. Because I saw it with my own eyes." Let's just say that there is a similar ring to Bachi Karkaria and Birinchi Baba.

But there's more to it than the names. While BB may have dreamed up his dealings with great men from different eras, BK has her own innate talent for stretching facts, knitting truths, half-truths and fiction into one colourful sweater, adding fistfuls of salt to bring to your table a slurpy, delicious soup from the Times of India kitchen. So what emerges in this book is a mythology, where facts gleefully, shamelessly tumble and play with fiction. Revel in the great sense of rumour that taps into this humour-mongering machine. Realize that as you turn every page that you needn't bother about whether an editor really had ten heads, or whether a Times-traveller brought home the Golden Fleece.

As Birinchi Baba would have expounded to a non-gullible audience, this book expresses Euhemerism: an approach that presumes that mythological accounts originate from real events and characters, but then turn mythic as they are retold, exaggerated, tweaked – and, in this case, passed through the Bachi Distillery. So, wise reader, believe and doubt with equal poise as you pass through the Times. Bachi as your chuckling tour guide won't have it any other way.

September 2016 — Indrajit Hazra

New Delhi

I

introduction

“You have to think of your brand as a kind of myth. A myth is a compelling story that is archetypal, if you know the teachings of Carl Jung. It has to have emotional content and all the themes of a great story: mystery, magic, adventure, intrigue, conflicts, contradiction, paradox.”

– Deepak Chopra –

Introduction

JOURNEY TO THE HEART OF A UNIVERSE

Arriving every morning as a trainee, I would pause at the portico in a self-conscious preen, signalling my insider status to those fated only to the periphery.

My first memory of the *Times of India* is that of people looking into it. There would always be a motley crowd on the pavement outside peering in through the glass and mesh, riveted to the frenetic roar of the rotary machine. One storey high and one block long, it swallowed reels of paper at the one end, and spat them out at the other in a stack of multicoloured sheets fluttering down with the lightness of butterflies. The four-page forms would disappear into some mysterious cavern to complete their metamorphosis into magazines: the crowd would tear itself away, and fresh reels and fresh groups would replace the earlier ones. It was a continuous process inside and outside, an unbroken cycle as constant as the flow of news.

One storey high and one block long, it [rotary machine] swallowed reels of paper at one end, and spat them out at the other in a stack of multicoloured sheets fluttering down with the lightness of butterflies.

Arriving every morning as a trainee, I would pause at the portico in a self-conscious preen, signalling my insider status to those fated only to the periphery. I would then have to sprint up, praying that I would catch the attendance register on time, and not have to grovel before the petty clerk imbued with the power of the red cross. Yes, even the anointed ones must bow to ritual.

Over the years, my entry lost its swagger as routine dulled the stage lights. Even the crowds found no reason to stand and gape because the machine itself moved away to a hi-tech printing facility in a faraway suburb; the ATM and the offices which took its place could not elicit the same reverence. But that roaring beast and the huddle of wide-eyed worshippers has remained a totem of the power of the *Times of India*. Awesome even when invisible.

Those on the outside must wonder what goes on inside this mythic media group. Something so simultaneously massive and mobile cannot be just a lifeless automaton, can it? Is it some monster god like that old machine, or failingly, touchingly, reassuringly human? Does it get indigestion from that gluttonous appetite? Does it have to slip into a subtle pranayam to still its restless mind? Does its spine give way like that of an action hero? Does it have a soul or is it quite happy to be a monopoly?

JOURNEY TO THE HEART OF A UNIVERSE

The Times of India is not a conglomerate of the media on its marquee, but of roles. For millions it is not just a news dispenser. It is at once protagonist and observer, wake-up call and lullaby, parent, child and sexed-up lover, creator, preserver and saboteur. Those on the outside must wonder some more. Does it do unto its own what it does to others? Can it keep up with itself; or what heavy-duty pacemakers are embedded deep inside? Does this unapologetic Midas have a beating heart, or is that too made of cold, hard gold?

These are existential questions. And they can be answered with theology or with mythology. I don't want to go into the first. I would rather tell you some of the stories instead. They are just a random selection taken from just 47 years of a 178-year-old epic, but they might help you understand the what, how and why of the TOI.

THE RED SWIVEL CHAIR

So, whenever someone went out for a longish meeting or lunch, he had to take the precaution of securing his chair to his desk with a bicycle chain lest some chairless colleague pull it up to his own table in the interim.

Aspiration would get straight A's. It became the key selling point of the *Times of India* and its solar system. Around 1985, the mother company, Bennett, Coleman & Co Ltd (BCCL), began dramatically altering its spin, and the revolution was well in place by the time of the 150-year jubilee which came shortly after. Pre-empting the economic reforms by seven years, it made the itch to be richer, smarter and higher acceptable, desirable, indeed inevitable. Readers flocked to it for a DIY guide to the professional and social galaxy.

I've arrived
.... ouch.

But aspiration wasn't invented by BCCL. It is as old as the fig leaf of Eden. Even in the years of socialist dormancy, individuals did not lose the gleam in their eye. Corporates provided their own metaphors of attainment.

THE RED SWIVEL CHAIR

The Red Swivel Chair was a universal symbol of Having Arrived, and it was duly coveted in the management halls of the historic TOI building on Mumbai's DN Road and the much newer Times House on Delhi's Bahadurshah Zafar Marg. Branches did not count. Editorial corridors had their own allegories.

The RSC was the corporate Mount Kailash, and every starry-eyed, young manager looked up to it in awestruck aspiration. You attained it only when you had reached the covenanted grade of Rs 600-Rs 1000. By the early 1970s, each chair was at least 15 to 20 years old, and all the four legs of its base were of a different shade because they had been replaced at different times.

Matters had come to such a pass because replacing the august red chair needed nothing short of a board sanction. And before the board would deign to consider such a move, no less a personage than the Chief Engineer had to solemnly declare in writing and in triplicate that the red chair in question was 'irreparable'. Since the framework was of wood, repairs could technically go on to infinity.

Constant salvage resulted in damage worse than mismatched legs. The coveted 'lal kursi' became such an ergonomic disaster that it invariably affected the cervical spine. But a red chair was a red chair, and the mighty sat on it in grandeur – and spondylitis. Yes, the surgical collar soon became as much a part of corporate regalia as the business suit. It was the price you paid for being bestowed the burden of high office. If the RSC was often shaky as well, that too could be a metaphor for your position.

One rung lower was the green chair. Nothing physically distinguished it from its red superior other than the colour of the rexine. But in management iconography, the chasm was huge. Green was merely for the supervisory grade.

Those who weren't even in this category did not have to worry about their spines. Instead they had to worry about having any chair at all. At times, there weren't enough for everybody. So, whenever someone went out for a longish meeting or lunch, he had to take the precaution of securing his chair to his desk with a bicycle chain lest some chairless colleague pull it up to his own table in the interim. No point in arguing with its new occupant. Possession, after all, is nine-tenth of the law, and the rule of 'Finders sitters' was non-negotiable.

But aspiration wasn't invented by BCCL.
It is as old as the fig leaf of Eden.
Even when it was forced into a larger dormancy,
individuals did not lose the gleam in their eye.
Corporates provided their own metaphors
of attainment.

In aspiration mythology, the RSC was rivalled only by the DLR …

IN FOR LUNCH

You have to be invited to it [Directors' Lunch Room] in a formal letter signed by the Chairman, or at least the GM.

Design makeovers have taken the sheen away from the red swivel chair, but the Directors' Lunch Room (DLR) is the abiding symbol of corporate nirvana. In both Mumbai and Delhi, it is positioned closer to the Management halls than those of Editorial.

This is not just an accident of berth. As in all newspaper offices, the two sides were arrayed against each other like mythic armies. The clink of china is merely the echo of epic battles past.

The DLR privilege is granted to both. However, the soldiers of neither side can just start sauntering in as soon as they achieve a certain rank. You have to be invited to it in a formal letter signed by the Chairman, or at least the GM. As in a lot of corporate offices, till the late 1970s, lunch was a proper sit-down affair with liveried waiters serving you at the long table. Today you stand balancing your plate, but the soup, salad, dessert, fresh fruit and elaborate vegetarian fare in chafing dishes remain.

IN FOR LUNCH

The DLR in the hoary Mumbai building is naturally more marinated in mystique. Today's cocky generation is blasé, but in the past, the lesser mortals in the management hall outside would watch the gods walk grandly in through its grand teak door. All the upper echelons reinforced their superiority every afternoon with this ritual. It was de rigeur as well because they were expected to continue business over lunch. Editorial, as usual, asserted its individuality.

Till the late 1980s, the DLR was a male club, the only qualifying woman being Vimla Patil who had taken over from 'Doc' Jhangiani as editor of Femina. She wasn't easily intimidated, but she chose to have a tray sent up to her 4th floor cabin. The voices were loud, the jokes bawdy, the laughter duly lusty, more so after Khushwant Singh became editor of the *Illustrated Weekly of India*.

The DLR in the hoary Mumbai building is naturally more marinated in mystique.

The Sardar had strong competition in Dr Dharam Vir Bharti, the literally and figuratively towering editor of *Dharmyug*. Each afternoon, he made a backdoor entry, taking the backstairs which were closer to his own 4th floor office. He would come in with his typical measured stride and raw silk bush shirt, a cigar dangling from his lips.

Sham Lal never came to the DLR since he ate books for lunch. He would go over to graze at Strand Book Stall, and engage in literary exchanges with its owner TN Shanbag, who became as much of a legend as the pageant of greats who passed through the organized chaos of his book shop off PM Road.

Girilal Jain, who succeeded Sham Lal as editor of the TOI, too was an infrequent member of the DLR. When he wasn't at Strand or a lunch engagement, he too would call for a tray.

Sham Lal never came to the DLR since he ate books for lunch.

The Mumbai DLR was an august institution, and as Pradeep Guha, later the boss of Response, himself admitted, "Chinnen Das and I were the first bandicoots to infiltrate into it. We were the Young Turks, and when we were inducted into this snooty club, you could have cut the hostility with a knife. But it was such a kick, sitting at the high table and dining with the very gods whose entry and exit we had earlier just watched from our lowly desks in the hall outside."

'Things done by halves are always done right.'

HALF TIMES

An august occupant of the coveted Red Swivel Chair in Mumbai was the lean, lanky, unsmiling T Pithavala, who later became Business Director. One of the lessons learnt early by the young Pradeep Guha was that when dealing with him, you should always ask for twice the quantity of what you required, and quote twice the price. He would slash the requisition order with all his bequeathed might, clearly believing that 'Things done by halves are always done right.'

In the '80s, all magazines were on life support. Everybody held the purse-strings very tightly and none more so than those who never knew the spelling of 'loosen' even in the heyday Times. People like Mr T for 'Take-half' Pithavala.

One of the lessons learnt early by the young Pradeep Guha was that when dealing with him, you should always ask for twice the quantity of what you required, and quote twice the price.

Fawzia Madni, the Response executive who was then handling most of the magazines, had to go to him begging for extra paper. On one occasion, she needed to add just four pages to the Weekly because a large and very welcome advertiser had been netted. The Business Director told her darkly, without even the ghost of a smile, "Miss Madni at this rate you are going to liquidate the company."

His ghost reportedly continued to stalk the administrative hall, arguably unsettled by the waste that had crept in unwatched by his beady eye.

He [Arun Arora] was offered a job when he didn't come looking for one, but his actual appointment looked as if it would get lost in a Dante-esque circle of interviews.

GETTING APPOINTED

Recruitments work out in unplanned ways at Bennett, but they often hit pay dirt. Arun Arora joined BCCL in 1969, worked here for over 30 years with one breakaway, and rose to become one of the non-Jain Big Three. The story of his coming on board the company is remarkable but not untypical. He was offered a job when he didn't come looking for one, but his actual appointment looked as if it would get lost in a Dante-esque circle of interviews.

Arora, 27, had been entrusted with resuscitating GD Birla's *Searchlight* in Patna which had been burned down by hooligans. He went to Delhi to ask Ramesh Chandra Jain, then manager of BCCL's Delhi office, for advice on machinery, etc. They chatted for a while, Ramesh-ji agreed to help, and as the young man was leaving, the obliging and avuncular gentleman bowled a googly. "How about joining us?" he said.

Patna to Delhi was very tempting, but young Arun said, "I can't even think of leaving till *Searchlight* is operational again." The senior man replied, "We're in no hurry. But we don't recruit just like that, so give me your CV." First an offer, then the high horse? The accidental recruit was bemused, and said he had never had occasion to make one. "Make it then, and send it," he was ordered.

Two months later, he got a call from Ramesh-ji. "Have you seen the advertisement we have put out for a production manager? Respond to it immediately." Arora did and was called for an interview three weeks later, with train fare provided. In Delhi, he was grilled by Ramesh Chandra, Dr Ram Tarneja, who was then the DGM, and three or four others. He was told, "We have shortlisted many applicants, so you will have to appear for several interviews." This was all getting a bit much, so Arora decided to lay down his own conditions: he wouldn't make the long train journey again, he would have to be given air fare. "And sufficient notice," he added.

A month and a half later, he was summoned to Mumbai with the promise of air-fare reimbursement. He awaited his turn on the famous red sofas outside the boardroom (they are still there, but they have emerged with more stylish upholstery after a later makeover). With him sat Purnendu Sen (who retired in 2009 as Director, Production) and PK Dey. They were already in TOI and had applied for this jump-up. They were dismissive about the outsider's chances, and said in their Bengali-Bambaiya mix, "Time khota karne ka nahin. You've got a return ticket, no?"

They looked as if they had been waiting to pounce on their prey. It also looked like it would be a slow, painful killing.

Once inside, the atmosphere was intimidating. A boardroom packed for the Grand Inquisition, and the brooding dark mahogany panelling didn't help either. The government –appointed Chairman Bedekar, Tarneja, Personnel Manager VG Karnik, Labour Manager Patil, the technical guys Krishnan and Bhasin and even the finance head. They looked as if they had been waiting to pounce on their prey. It also looked like it would be a slow, painful killing.

GETTING APPOINTED

They were all being pompous and showing off, but young Arora soon realised that they knew little about technology. He knew much more than his years on the job suggested. At *Searchlight* he had ended up handling everything because his boss was a retired director of education in the Patna secretariat, and preferred to spend the day reading fiction. So Arora had taken charge of circulation, advertising, production, purchase, the works.

The interview was for production manager, but no technology-related questions were put. Instead, he was asked how he would better manage newsprint. That too was easy because he had worked out the system. Newsprint was a controlled commodity. It was imported by the State Trading Corporation, and doled out according to quotas. There were no weighing machines and a rough rule of thumb was three reels to a ton. The wrappers were torn off and sold as 'raddi'. The smaller papers had worked out their deals with the junior officers, and the worst newsprint was left for *The Statesman*, followed by TOI – since the latter was temporarily in government 'hands', typically no one cared.

Anyway the two technical guys seemed impressed, and the Labour Manager followed Arora out of the room and congratulated him for his excellent showing. Then he added a note of caution, "But that doesn't mean you should put in your papers at *Searchlight*. In *Times of India*, until such time as you don't have written confirmation in a letter signed by the Personnel Manager, you cannot assume that the job is yours."

The interview was for production manager, but no technology-related questions were put.

It was two months before The Letter arrived, and he was ordered to join in seven days. By now, *Searchlight* was up and running again, but he couldn't just walk away. He asked for three months, they agreed on a month and a half. Arun Arora joined in Delhi. It was a full year since Ramesh Chandra Jain had offered him a job.

The Times of India
had been started,
failed and shut down.
Many of the former staff were
still looking for jobs getting
scarcer in a pariah market,
so the company wasn't exactly
Miss Popularity.

TALES FROM THE FRONTIER

No one expected the Punjabi Arun Arora to launch into a Rabindrasangeet when he was asked to move to Kolkata to start a second Economic Times edition there some time after he'd joined TOI as Production Manager in Delhi. But he didn't break into a bhangra either. Industrial unrest leading to the flight of capital was turning the once commercial capital of the Raj back into Kipling's 'city of darkest night', literally too courtesy the sweltering power cuts known as loadshedding.

The branch was something of a Black Hole of Calcutta too. *The Times of India* had been started, failed and shut down. Many of the former staff were still looking for jobs getting scarcer in a pariah market, so the company wasn't exactly Miss Popularity. But Ashok Jain was keen to have a publishing presence in the city of the family's industrial springboard.

The company acquired a creaky building on SN Banerjee Road. It was formerly an 'adda-ghar', the 'hang-out' space of the young swains of old Calcutta families set apart from the proper ancestral 'baari'; it even had a discreetly concealed back entrance for dancing girls. In their place had arrived a creakier printing machine bought off Chhatra Parishad, the student wing of the Congress party. Not only was it as geriatric as a political leader, it had been cannibalized of all its brass parts. This double whammy apart, its cut-off, that is, image area, did not match the cut-off of the mother ET in Bombay. But the board was in no mood to import a new machine, certainly not for iffy Kolkata. Yet, Ashok-ji's emotional attachment could not be ignored either.

Thoughts turned to the bright young techno whiz. The GM, Dr Ram S Tarneja, called Arun Arora from Bombay HQ and asked, "How did you salvage the *Searchlight* machines? Can you do the same for the one we have in Calcutta?" Arora stated the obvious: "I can tell you only after I've had a look." Then Ramesh Chandra put a spanner in the works, saying he did not want to lose his production manager.

When young AA examined the machine, he realized that his problems would be more political than technical. He told Dr Tarneja, "It's do-able, but please sort it out with my boss." Ramesh-ji relented, "Bhai, doctor ko kaise manaa kar sakte hain?"

So, to a hiss of amazement in Delhi, the young man leapfrogged over several seniors, and found himself installed as branch head. He also got an invitation to SP Jain's august lunch room in the Rohtas Industries office on tony Camac Street. The paterfamilias of the empire was as intrigued by the unconventional appointment.

Glory is all very well, but what about the gritty, to say nothing of the nitty? The following stories will find echoes in the frontier lore of all companies especially in times when they resembled the 'licence raj' bureaucracy they were pitted against.

TALES FROM THE FRONTIER

The Kolkata operation had to be very hush-hush lest newspaper rivals use it to instigate the earlier and still-disgruntled staff, so no recruitment ads could be released. And, even if they found candidates, Cal branch could only shortlist. Mumbai HQ controlled all interviews and appointments.

With both hands and half a leg tied, Arora managed to find jobpress men and trained them for newspaper production. The Marxist Jyoti Basu, recently anointed Chief Minister, inaugurated Calcutta's new business paper.

Arora and his team came to the event straight from the press where they had spent all night getting the literal and figurative nuts and bolts in place. Seeing them in their shirt sleeves, and crumpled ones at that, the sartorially propah Dr Tarneja gasped aghast: "Nanga aa gaye ho! (You've come naked!)." Arora did possess a solitary jacket but it was at home in faraway Lake Town. His colleague Ram Hingorani didn't even own one, but he was quicker on the draw and borrowed a spare one from Dr Rangnekar, the editor who had flown in from Mumbai and still had his suitcase with him. Arora had to make a dash to Park Street to dip into his cousin's wardrobe. And in their borrowed plumes, the Kolkata ET took wing.

Okay, the job-press men had joined, been trained, been persuaded to get on with their tasks despite the fact that they had no appointment letters. (Naturally, their new boss did not pass on the cautionary advice that he had received a little over a year ago from BCCL's Labour Manager.) The time to pay their first salaries arrived. But not those crucial signed letterheads.

In despair, the young manager went to Narendra Kumar, who himself was the youngest board director of Bennett, and a big cup in the tea business. From him Arora got his second piece of sage advice. "Yeh Times-waley court se bahut dartey hain. They abhor getting into legal wrangles. Ek chitthi zaroor daal do, send them a letter warning them that if salaries are not paid rightaway, there is real danger of a gherao and prolonged industrial action."

You have to remember that these were the years of militant trade-unionism, and violent workers would often put petrified managers under siege, sometimes fatally. It became so rampant, that 'gherao' passed into the *Oxford English Dictionary*. Moreover, the company had already badly burnt its fingers once before in Kolkata. The appointment letters came pronto.

The problem of filing cabinets remained. Arora needed seven, he was given only two, and the remaining files were piled on the floor of his room. Containing confidential material, they couldn't be dumped elsewhere. When he indented for more, the Accounts babu said, 'Filing cabinets are a capital item. You are not entitled to authorize them. Only the board can sanction."

"Yeh Times-waley court se bahut dartey hain. They abhor getting into legal wrangles. Ek chitthi zaroor daal do, send them a letter warning them that if salaries are not paid rightaway, there is real danger of a gherao and prolonged industrial action."

"So, what can I authorize?" asked the frustrated Branch Head. "Only a stool, saar," was the bland reply. But the accountant helpfully guided him on how to draft the note to ensure swift passage past the bureaucracy.

The problem of filing cabinets remained.
Arora needed seven, he was given only two,
and the remaining files
were piled on the floor of his room.
Containing confidential material,
they couldn't be dumped elsewhere.

TALES FROM THE FRONTIER

Ramesh Chandra Jain was now the director for Kolkata, but he couldn't help his former protégée on this business of cabinets. He was authorized to sanction only up to Rs 30,000 of capital expenses, and all this was used up because such a huge backlog had piled up in Delhi during the years that the company was in the control of government-appointed directors. "Ek do sey kaam chala lo, manage with one or two," he told Arora.

However, by the time Arora left the branch two and a half years later, all the records were safely ensconced in filing cabinets.

Anyone involved in startups might sniff, "Big deal. Tell us something new. All this is par for the course." Okay. Try matching the story of The Gate.

Yes, the ET had acquired a grand if dilapidated mansion, but it had no gate. One could not be put up either because a paan-cigarette-wallah had installed himself at the entrance to the compound. A solution would have to be found. Through Chief Minister Jyoti Basu's amenable son, Chandan, a fixer called 'Prince' Gupta was contacted. He considered the problem and then said firmly, "Boldly kaam kortey hobey". (The job will have to be accomplished boldly.) You dismantle his shop, I will ensure that no one from the police station intervenes. But do this and complete your gate in three hours. After that I won't be responsible for any consequences."

Arora knew that if he sought official permission from HQ to set up a gate, there would be the usual 'note-baji', then the matter would turn into a civil suit and get stuck interminably in the court. He chose Prince Gupta's Cinderella option.

He commandeered the toughies whom he had employed from the small presses and told them to deal with the paanwalla and keep any meddlesome locality 'dadas' at bay. His instructions

He [Prince Gupta] commandeered the toughies whom he had employed from the small presses and told them to deal with the paanwalla and keep any meddlesome locality 'dadas' at bay. His instructions were, "No violence. But get the job done."

were, “No violence. But get the job done.” The fellow protested when he saw the menacing posse approaching, “I’ve been here from my baap-dada ka time, I’ll call the police.” Ignoring him, they transferred his stuff to the pavement outside, bodily lifted him off his squat, pulled him screaming and kicking into the building, and pushed him into the room kept for visiting directors.

Arora arrived and told him that he had nothing to worry about if he left the premises quietly. He then asked him the value of his goods. His stall was just a wooden stand with betel leaves and their stuffing plus a garland of cigarette boxes, But he said, “Rs 5,000.” The senior guys pooled their own resources. Then the paanwalla whined, “I’ll have to go back to my village near Kanpur. Give me the train fare plus what I’ll need to eat on the way. Rs 250 will do.”

He was given the money, but made to sign a letter saying that he had sold his shop to BCCL and received ‘full and final settlement’. Arora told his toughies to escort him to the tenement where he lived, get him to pack his belongings, and not let him out of their sight till he had boarded the train. In the meanwhile, the company’s contractor swiftly installed the gate. The operation was over within the three-hour quota, with three minutes to spare. Mumbai HQ never got to know the details of this operation.

Arora, however, did get into trouble over his next piece of enterprise. Realising that the once-dud-now-refurbished machine had idle capacity, the enthusiastic manager thought they could easily produce an evening paper. He had it designed, and even printed 100 dummy copies. When he proudly air-bagged them to Mumbai, Dr Tarneja hollered at him over the phone. “You fool! Who authorized you? Only the board can make such a decision. We designated you Branch manager only for technical reason, but you are actually just a Press Manager.”

He ordered him, "Burn the copies, burn the mats, and make sure that no news of this stupidity leaks out."

When Arora tried to stammer out the explanation about excess capacity, he was promptly ticked off again. "That's not your headache. We don't want any innovations." More than three decades later, Arora could still hear Dr T's admonition ringing in his ears, "We are the thinkers, you just be the doer. Is that clear?"

TALES FROM THE FRONTIER

Yes, the early years of the Kolkata ET were as volatile as the city beyond its infamous gate. Just as in the bars there was 'Never a night without a fight', in the fledgling edition there was 'Never a night without a fright'. Take the unorthodox business of the Nolan Caster. This was a critical piece of equipment needed to cast the hot lead from the papier mache mats for the blocks used in printing advertisements. They had only one, and there would be no edition if it conked off. It did.

Arora, veteran of Operation Searchlight Salvage, had learnt much about make-do and makeshift. As the machine groaned to a halt, and could not be revived, the boss did not follow suit.

Just as in the bars there was 'Never a night without a fight', in the fledgling edition there was 'Never a night without a fright'.

He sent out a peon to buy a large karhai, the deep wok used by corner halwais, and a bucket stove on which the city's poor routinely cooked their dinner. They lit the sigdi, perched the karhai atop it, melted the lead and with the long-handled karchhi, which had been bought along with the wok, ladled it on to the mats. Voilà it worked.

The low-tech solution was deployed for two days till a call came from Dr T. He demanded, "How are you producing a paper without a Nolan Caster?" Arora hemmed, hawed and replied, "We have made indigenous arrangements, Sir." Forced to spell them out, he again got into hot water, or hot lead. "Are you crazy? Do you know how poisonous lead fumes are? We could face industrial action. This is the *Times of India*, not your *Searchlight*."

The fire died down, but the joke did not. For several years after that, his Mumbai colleagues sniggered and called him 'the karhaiwalla'. The production bosses, however, appreciated both his predicament and his solution. They commiserated, "If you have a problem, just tell us. We'll help you out." And ET Kolkata got a second Nolan Caster.

There is one more story from those old days, and the guy in trouble this time was not the Branch Head but the Personnel Manager. This gentleman was a Goan bodybuilder, a huge man with formidable pecs. All appointment letters came from head office, all HR issues were sorted out there too, and there was no industrial unrest here unlike in so many other West Bengal establishments. So, Mr Goa had much time on his hands. He would disappear to the typically Kolkata flat-roofed terrace of the ET building to indulge in his favourite pastime: flying kites.

The workers decided to play a prank, and locked the small door of the terrace while he was up there. The watchman, party to the joke, pretended not to hear his frantic cries. He was rescued late in the evening when Arora, returning from some calls, saw him desperately waving.

Arora warned him with the 'Bombay HQ Bogey': "They will find out!" That was deterrent enough. Personnel Manager henceforth did not tell himself – or anyone else – to 'Go fly a kite'.

And here is a story from the editorial side of the start-up

Gautam Adhikari worked for the State Bank of India in Kolkata but his heart was in journalism. Darryl D'Monte, then an Assistant Editor hot out of Cambridge and with Marxist views, had helped him to get an article published in the TOI. This was the first time that his byline had appeared in a major national publication, instead of the usual left-wing paper. To be Bengali was to be an intellectual, and to be an intellectual was to be left-wing in those times. It is still so, since the east will always be red.

TALES FROM THE FRONTIER

Gautam had scouted around at *The Statesman* and the *Ananda Bazar Patrika's* English paper *Hindustan Standard*, but "nobody would take me because newspapers didn't pay even the then lowly banking salaries. I was willing to take a salary cut, but they refused to entertain such a suspect offer." Then he heard that ET was coming to Kolkata, and immediately called Darryl, his old and sole contact in the Times Group. "Is it true?" asked G. "Yes, why don't you apply?" suggested D.

Gautam did, got called for an interview and found himself at that dilapidated, old mansion. The broad staircase shook when he trudged up, and he wasn't sure if it was "because of the neglected building or because of my nervous legs".

The interview was held in a room of seedy grandeur with the ET editor, Dr D.K. Rangnekar, and the Personnel Manager (the more high-falutin HR hadn't been heard of then) B.G. Karnik, flanking the august GM, Dr Ram Tarneja.

"You know banking, that's good for us, but you are mad to leave a well-paid job when you have a wife and a new baby," said Rangnekar, echoing what Nihal Singh at the Statesman and Aveek Sarkar at ABP had told him. Gautam brashly replied, "If you want to take me, tell me. Otherwise I'm quitting SBI tomorrow and joining *The Statesman* or maybe the *Hindustan Standard*."

The next day, he got a phone call to come and discuss the terms, and he found to his amazed delight that he was being given almost as much as his current bank salary.

"Kunal Bose and I were the two reporters, Krishnaswamy was the Chief of Bureau, and that was the sum total of the editorial team of the new edition of the *Economic Times*.

To be Bengali was to be an intellectual, and to be an intellectual was to be left-wing in those times. It is still so, since the east will always be red.

"With our jhola slung from our right shoulder, umbrella in hand, we would wade through Kolkata's flooded roads. Among them, was the aptly named Waterloo Street. Kunal and I covered all the commercial sectors as well as the Assembly. We worked our butts off, also taking in three or four press conferences, returning to the flaking office to hammer out our stories on the old Remingtons and Olivettis. After 6 to 8 months, enough confidence in the paper had been built up for Mumbai HQ to sanction an expansion of staff.

Rangnekar was the first in a lineage of brilliant ET editors. He was quiet till you managed to get him one-on-one on a subject that fired him. The small team would be on tenterhooks whenever he visited Kolkata. On such an occasion, Gautam got talking to him on the state of the economy and the world, and Rangnekar called him to continue the conversation over a drink at the Ritz Hotel on Chowringhee where he was staying.

The Editor still had on his tie, but loosened. He pulled out the distinctive bottle of Camus V.S.O.P from his suitcase. The young reporter's eyes widened because he had only heard of it. Said Gautam, "Rangnekar sat nursing a single shot. And we had one of the greatest conversations of my life. I didn't know then that he was about to quit to start *Business Standard*."

Ahmedabad

Some people never learn, and Arun Arora took his enterprise/ insubordination with him to his next posting, this one at the other end of the subcontinent's breadth, in Ahmedabad, where there was no

ET, but the *Times of India*. It was already up and running, so he did not have to play midwife as in Kolkata. But there was still labour and pains because the TOI there was bleeding.

The edition had been losing money ever since it had been started some 12 years earlier. This was not surprising considering that, because of its low circulation – and a price-sensitive market – the rate for classified advertisements was only Rs 2.50.

One day an NRI Patel barged into his office, and said, "I came here to put in an ad. I am going back without doing so. Do you know why, Mr Manager? I will tell you. I came to your office from Kankaria in a rickshaw (a three-wheeler). It cost me Rs 3, and your ad costs only Rs 2.50. What kind of response will it get?"

The incorrigible Arora again 'overstepped' his authority, and straightaway doubled the rate. Then, emboldened, increased it to Rs 7. He didn't bother with the detail of informing the Advertising Manager at Mumbai HQ, 'Terror' Thirumalai. Classifieds started building up, and his 'lapse' came to light only when questions began to be raised over how Ahmedabad was suddenly making profits.

There was a huge ruckus because what is sent up can't be brought down. Going by the law of the mille rate, Mumbai and Delhi, with their bigger circulations, were obliged to raise theirs. Not a bad thing for the bottom-line, but a pain in the same anatomical vicinity for those who had to go out and sell at this forcibly raised rate.

Once again, he was far from gently reminded of what he could do and what he could not do. And Arora once again learnt what several managers holding the fort in outposts have before and since: doing what you think is good for the company plays havoc with the omnipotent system. No ex-gratia award for guessing who wins.

II

the mother ship

"I believe that imagination is stronger than knowledge. That myth is more potent than history. That dreams are more powerful than facts. That hope always triumphs over experience. That laughter is the only cure for grief. And I believe that love is stronger than death."

– **Robert Fulghum** –

The world was trapped
in a maelstrom of rival power blocs,
and India itself was going through
extreme turbulence
in its search for an identity.

EPIC HEROES

"There was an epic dimension to the eccentricities of old-time editors. The world was trapped in a maelstrom of rival power blocs, and India itself was going through extreme turbulence in its search for an identity. But as soon as GDP broke free of the so-called Hindu rate of growth, an intellectual dullness crept in because the Great Grappling was over. Media is flourishing to a once unimaginable degree, but with 'feedback', 'leveraging' and 'brand-building' has come a depersonalization, the ironing out of eccentricities, and the 'characters' who once gave the august corridors such a declaiming, despairing, delicious ring." – Dileep Padgaonkar

Frank Moraes, NJ Nanporia and Sham Lal had distinct personalities, even intellectual snobbery, but no overbearing arrogance. That would come only with the imperious Girilal Jain. As

Dileep described him, "He was given to making Spenglarian statements covering vast ages and aeons in a single sentence. He was a blend of Curzonian ambitions and Haryanvi conceits." No surprise then that when he went to Iran to interview the Shah, he is supposed to have ended up tutoring the Pahlavi monarch on matters of geo-political strategy.

Of an evening, Giri would walk in the Lodhi Gardens, that Mount Parnassus of Delhi's intellectual and cultural pantheon, puff at his cigar and come up with statements that would flummox even the lofty companion he had chosen. He would pronounce, "The Hun will be pitted against the Hindu." Then, after a cogitating pause, he would elaborate, as dusk bathed the tombs in ochre light and parrots painted the deepening sky in streaks of raucous green.

"He [Laxman] was given to making Spenglarian statements covering vast ages and aeons in a single sentence. He was a blend of Curzonian ambitions and Haryanvi conceits."

The most notable feature of the creator of the common man was that he was completely lacking in the common touch.

THE UNCOMMON MAN

The most notable feature of the creator of the common man was that he was completely lacking in the common touch. To all but a close circle of personal friends and a coterie of the editors he worked with, RK Laxman was arrogant to the point of rudeness. Forget about not tolerating fools, he didn't tolerate anyone who wasn't in the vicinity of his intellectual altitude. Only part of it can be attributed to his typical Tam-Brahm cynicism.

Was it a front to be able to work with the degree of concentration his art required, to island himself in a daily newspaper's natural state of turbulence? Let us say 'perhaps', and let it rest at that. Genius, national treasure, indisputably the greatest Indian cartoonist and one with an unparalleled body of work that never faltered in its incisive comment or draughtsmanship every single day. In a man such as this, arrogance must be not just forgiven, but expected. It is his noblesse oblige.

Laxman came in to work at 8.30 am sharp, driving his own black Ambassador and parking it in the same place. No one would dare to appropriate it, even if he had arrived early enough to do so. And if someone tried reversing into that hallowed space in blissful ignorance of the heresy he was about to commit, a posse of alarmed TOI security men would surge out to shoo him away.

The other peons may not have begun their tasks of dusting, clearing, laying out fresh water and newspapers, but Laxman's Shetty would be there even earlier than his boss to ensure that the pencils were sharpened, that the pad on the table-top sketching stand was turned to a clean sheet and that all that morning's dailies had been screwed into their set place on his personal newspaper stand along the wall.

In a man such as this, arrogance must be not just forgiven, but expected. It is his noblesse oblige.

By the time the assistant editors and editors assembled for their 10.30 am meeting, Laxman's cartoon had gestated in his head, and had perhaps birthed in a first draft on his pad. Laxman would saunter-stride into the meeting, a part of it and yet apart. In the TOI hierarchy, he was in a niche of his own on par with that of the editor.

In later years – I would like to add 'mellower' but it wouldn't be true and moreover Laxman would disdainfully disapprove – he would regale the awed assembly with stories of past legendary editors, told with a droll, deadpan wit. If he was in an exceptionally good mood, he would wind up the tale with one of his coin tricks. That's why his bush shirt had those deep, low pockets. White bush shirt, black trousers. No one can recall Laxman in anything else. Arguably not even his wife Kamala, as friendly as Laxman was prickly.

Laxman was a man of many moods, mercurial, impatient, ebullient one moment, ill-tempered the other. He could make people laugh, yes, but he could reduce them to tears with equal glee. Even less known than his sleight of hand with coins was his fantastic gift of mimicry. True, all cartoonists must have a heightened sense of observation, but not all can act out the quirks they have so keenly noticed and captured in a cartoon or caricature. When so inclined, he kept his friends and colleagues in splits with perfectly pitched imitations.

THE UNCOMMON MAN

Even his observations were 'astounding' to use the adjective of Dileep Padgaonkar with whom he worked on a book on Maharashtra, travelling for days at a stretch across the state. The cartoonist told the writer, "You will always see two things. In the towns, whenever a man is walking down the road with a child, the child will always be on the side closer to traffic instead of the other way around." Dileep looked at him cynically and was told, "Ok, you see for yourself." The first 10 duos they came across bore out Laxman's point. Case closed.

His second observation was that in every village there would be at least one very old person wearing soda-bottle lens glasses. Sure enough, there always was, the result of cataract surgery in the days and places which didn't know about implanted lenses.

True, all cartoonists must have a heightened sense of observation, but not all can act out the quirks they have so keenly noticed and captured in a cartoon or caricature.

Dileep told a tale from another trip. Laxman and Kamala had gone to Qatar as guests of the sheikh. A public lecture was part of the deal. The opening line of his speech left his audience and his princely host stunned. He said, "Ever since I have set foot in your country, I have been most unhappy, in fact downright miserable."

He then went on, "If a car is to pick me up at 10, it is always there at five to 10, with the AC switched on. I never have to open the door, the smartly uniformed chauffeur has always jumped out to do this for me. My heart sinks every time I drive through your country. The ride is always smooth with none of the potholes I am used to back home, Every street light is working. The walls are clean without a single blob of betel juice. How do you expect me, a person from Bombay, not to feel totally depressed about this?"

"I zimply told them, 'Not today, not today. Today's my Wednesday vow.' In India, the safest way to escape is by using religion."

The crowd cracked up with laughter and he had them eating out of his hand for the rest of the evening.

Laxman and Dileep had also travelled to Patna together. At every event, the renowned cartoonist was mobbed by crowds, and a posse of policemen had to be deputed to control them. He adored the adulation, but then got irritated. It seemed as if he had done nothing but inaugurate exhibitions throughout that two-day trip. He tried to wriggle out of the last one, but the eager organisers said, "Sir, please, it will be over in five minutes." Laxman turned to Dileep and hissed, "I zay, it's never going to be over in five minutes. There will be garlands, flowery speeches, photographs, and presentation of 'momentoes'. But watch me."

He cut the ribbon, and whizzed out saying something to his taken-aback hosts. "How did you do it?" asked a bemused and impressed Dileep. "I zimply told them, 'Not today, not today. Today's my Wednesday vow.' In India, the safest way to escape is by using religion."

Gautam Adhikari also had the pleasure of travelling with Laxman. The cartoonist had been invited to Boston by *Daedalus* magazine published by the MIT press, while Gautam was at Harvard. And since Gautam and his wife Rita were driving to New York, he took a ride with them.

THE UNCOMMON MAN

"I have never had such a side-splitting four hours in my life. At times I had to pull the car off the highway and stop, I was laughing so hard. He regaled us with stories, jokes, gossip."

There had been a plane accident somewhere that morning, in which the roof had mysteriously blown off. Laxman gave his straight-faced version of how the plane suddenly became a convertible, what happened to the air hostess as she was pouring the tea, etc etc. painting the whole incident as a hilarious farce, and periodically shaking his head and saying, "It's sad. Very sad."

The cartoonist [Laxman] used his sharp wit to come up with code names for the worthies on the other side of the virtual barrier separating editorial from management. Arora, as in Arun, was 'Borealis'.

Maybe because they were laughing so much, Gautam landed up in the Bronx which didn't look very hospitable. He was about to turn into a gas station with a big black attendant. Laxman said sounding every bit as if he meant it, "If you go in there, I'm going to jump out of the car. Just press on the accelerator and drive out of this place as soon as you can."

Laxman described the slick, black, heavily pomaded coiffure of Ghafoor Noorani, the eminent lawyer and frequent visitor to the TOI's Mumbai office, as 'patent leather hair'. That's exactly what it looked like.

In the same heritage building on DN Road, the cartoonist used his sharp wit to come up with code names for the worthies on the other side of the virtual barrier separating editorial from management. Arora, as in Arun, was 'Borealis'. (Mr Arora would get another, more good-humoured moniker when he joined Sony as its CEO with what was then an astounding Rs 1 crore p.a. package. At his farewell, a speaker cheekily commented, "There is no truth in the rumour that Mr Arora will henceforth be called Mr Carora.")

Certainly, Laxman had worked with more legendary greats than anyone around. He had started his career at *The Hindu* in his native Madras, then moved to Mumbai and *The Free Press Journal* with Bal Thackeray who continued to be both friend and unspared subject. Next he decided to take a shot at the TOI. " I was given an audience with Sir Francis Low – nice fellow, I zay – who told me 'We don't carry cartoons. But we can use you in *Evening News*.' Then, one day, he particularly liked one of my cartoons there, and said, 'This should have gone in the *Times of India*.' So I started doing work regularly for the morning paper." 'Regularly' soon became daily.

THE UNCOMMON MAN

Naturally, he got the opportunity to meet other legends. "Bertrand Russell told me 'Indians have discovered nothing', and quickly added with a twinkle in his eye, 'Don't look so angry young man. I meant they are the ones who discovered the concept of zero'."

Sir David Low was the self-taught New Zealander who moved to London and became arguably the 20th century's greatest political cartoonist and caricaturist. One day he walked into Laxman's cabin in the TOI, and said, "I loved your work right from the days you were at *The Hindu*. I am on my way to Hong Kong, and I simply had to stop by in Bombay to meet you." Laxman took him around. When they went to Malabar Hill, "I showed him the sweep of grand buildings along Marine Drive and said patronisingly to him, 'You people think India is a land of snake charmers. It's no such thing.' Just then, we heard the strains of a pipe playing, and there was a snake charmer. Low didn't say a word."

If you are impressed that Laxman met TS Eliot, let me tell you that it was arranged through Graham Greene, "a friend of my brother" – the celebrated novelist RK Narayan.

Did Laxman ever have a serious quarrel with the Indian editors who succeeded the British ones, Frank Moraes, NJ Nanporia, Sham Lal, Giri Lal? "Never. We held each other in great respect. Frank was a fine, gentle man. Yes, sometimes a bit high." Was it true that he would come into office reeling, and write his most hard-hitting editorials when drunk? "Nonsense, I zay, that is all nonsense," spluttered Laxman, his trademark disdain not in the least softened by the stroke he suffered in 2003. He gradually got back the use of his drawing arm, but his lines lacked their earlier subtle finesse. The message of the daily cartoon remained as incisive.

'We don't carry cartoons. But we can use you in Evening News. *' Then, one day, he [Sir Francis Low] particularly liked one of Laxman's cartoons there, and said, 'This should have gone in the* Times of India. *' So he started doing work regularly for the morning paper.' Regularly soon became daily.*

Laxman "sometimes accompanied Nanporia on his Sunday trips to Chor Bazar. He found a bargain almost every time. Images of gods and goddesses, furniture, even rare books – Nanporia and Sham Lal would be at Strand Book Stall every lunch time."

"The editors were all gentlemen. They would discuss books and authors over a drink in one another's houses." He did not add that the conversation included some not very intellectual gossip about politicians and peers. Girilal Jain, for instance, provided considerable grist to the rumour mill. In fact, when it stopped being mere rumour, it was a major factor in the unceremonious exit of a towering editor.

Gautam Adhikari confirmed that Giri did often boast that he was the 'secondmost important person in the country'. "We would joke behind his back, "So Sheshan (his secretary) is the 10th most important, and Bhagwati (his peon) is the 17th most important."

SECOND MOST IMPORTANT

Dileep Padgaonkar, TOI's homegrown, French-bred assistant editor, succeeded Girilal Jain, who was last full-fledged editor of the TOI. Henceforth, they would be designated executive editors. Like the more loudly flamboyant Pritish Nandy at the Weekly, Dileep was, in his colleague Dina Vakil's memorable phrase, 'an impresario editor'.

She drew out the syllables, very slowly, 'aam-pra-ssaa-ree-oh'.

Despite the pruning of the designation, this was the man who famously told an interviewer that he held 'the secondmost challenging job in the country'. The interviewer being Shobhaa De, and the magazine being *Society*, the preen was emblazoned across the cover. Embarrassed, 'Paddy' said he had actually quoted his imperious boss, Girilal Jain, but it was wrongly (mischievously?) attributed to him.

Secondmost
important job

Gautam Adhikari confirmed that Giri did often boast that he was the 'secondmost important person in the country'. "We would joke behind his back, "So Sheshan (his secretary) is the 10th most important, and Bhagwati (his peon) is the 17th most important."

SECONDMOST IMPORTANT

Dileep presided over a fine dining table and the TOI, many would aver, in that order.

One of the nuggets in the newsroom's annals is that the only time he sent out a memo, and one steeped in aged balsamic at that, was when the *Sunday Times of India* appeared with 'bouillabaisse' misspelt. For the Francophile and foodie editor it was a crime worse than a murdered filet mignon.

Since they meet more interesting people in their workaday world and because they have a mastery over words, most journalists can regale party companions with great stories. Their profession requires a close observation of their subjects, and a flair for mimicry is a delightful side-effect. In this league of engaging raconteurs, Dileep (also called Phillipe with Gaelic exaggeration) is to my mind incomparable in the spinning out a tale. It loses much in written prose but try to listen rather than to read as Paddy speaks in low deadpan tones but with mischief gambolling around his pursed rosebud lips. Let us hear him …

He [Sham Lal] turned pale
at the prospect of having
to handle [the baby] what for him
was no better than
an extra-terrestrial being,
and protested as emphatically
as he could.

LEGENDS OF SHAM LAL

Here are some of Dileep Padgaonkar's Sham Lal stories told in his incomparable after-dinner style. "Sham Lal came to Paris while I was posted there as TOI's correspondent. Our first son was just about a year old, and we begged him to 'babysit' for just an hour since Latika and I hadn't had the opportunity to go out at all for a quiet *dinner á deux* since Nikhil was born. Of course Sham Lal, the recluse who would not want to be left alone with most adults even of his close acquaintance, was hardly the companion of choice for a baby.

"He turned pale at the prospect of having to handle what for him was no better than an extra-terrestrial being, and protested as emphatically as he could. But we desperately wanted to go out, so we begged and pleaded and said, 'But he'll be fast asleep so you won't have to do anything at all; you can just keep reading.' We made it impossible for him to refuse this poor young couple. We had our relaxed dinner with a good wine, and strolled back.

LEGENDS OF SHAM LAL

"As soon as we entered the hallway of our building, we heard the baby and sprinted up the stairs to our flat. There was our Nikhil standing up in his bedroom cot holding on to the railing and bawling his head off. And out in the sitting room was Sham Lal, pacing up and down saying, 'Hell-oh, hell-oh, hell-oh!'

"What greater involvement could we have expected? You remember the fire story?" Yes, but tell, tell it again, the party audience pleads with Dileep. It doesn't take much pleading. "Sham Lal always took a ride back home with Inder Malhotra, who was quite used to driving while Sham Lal remained engrossed in his reading. One evening, there was a huge commotion on account of a big fire. Inder said, 'Good heavens, this building is on fire!' 'Is it?' said Sham Lal without looking up from his book."

He didn't cast a glance at the reality actually looking in at him. He was a prisoner of the printed word.

Sham Lal never ever noticed the beggars and the bright, little, singing, dancing 'No-Mama, No-Papa' kids who came knocking on Inder's car window at every traffic light either. That was the irony of the man who wrote so persuasively of India's pervasive poverty and the social injustice of not bringing development or even help to the marginalized. He didn't cast a glance at the reality actually looking in at him. He was a prisoner of the printed word.

Another of Dileep's Sham Lal in Paris stories was about the afternoon that they came home to the flat to find no sign of their house guest. The denizen of the ivory tower certainly would not have ventured out for an exploration of the Parisian streets. As Dileep recalled, "We looked everywhere. We thought he was in the loo. After 20 minutes, Latika knocked on the bathroom door and asked in a querulous voice, 'Sham Lal-ji, are you there?'

"And we heard a desultory 'Yes.' Another 15 minutes elapsed, and Sham Lal had not emerged. Now we were really worried, and pushed open the door. No one was inside. Ultimately we found him wedged between the window ledge and the back of the sofa, what else but engrossed in a book.

When Sham Lal retired, the newsroom (which he had never stepped into) gave him a farewell.

On another visit, DN Dhar, the Kashmir historian, and IG Patel, the economist, were also in town. Sham Lal convinced them that they should all go see an Ionesco play being staged by one of his Left Bank acquaintances. Dileep recalls, "After great effort, we located the obscure hall in the Latin Quarter. There was an audience of four, so the addition of our party really made it respectable. When the curtain opened, we found that the cast comprised the ticket seller, the man who had rung the starting bell, and the girl who had taken our coats at the entrance.

"The next day at lunch, Sham Lal held us all in thrall by waxing eloquent on not just Ionesco and the Theatre of the Absurd, but Godard and the other French greats of *cinema verite*."

Dileep added, "In the midst of this, one of these elevated intellects (and he refused to say which) interrupted to ask where he could see a blue movie." You can bet your last croissant that it wasn't Sham Lal.

And here's one more from the plebian side of The Corridor. When Sham Lal retired, the newsroom (which he had never stepped into) gave him a farewell. It was held in the 6th floor canteen where the aam janata, not 'invited' to the august Directors' Lunch Room, ate. Sham Lal

LEGENDS OF SHAM LAL

was seldom seen in the latter, so he probably did not even know of the existence of the former. He was escorted up in the lift and into the huge hall. The canteen has since undergone an impressive makeover of both furniture and fare, but those were still the days of aluminum benches and tables, dented thalis being rattled in the scullery, and cats and kittens mewing around.

News editor, chief reporter, subs, peons, all sung his fulsome praises. The quiet but universally admired editor was presented 'floral tributes' and a salver. Then the Master of Ceremonies grandly announced, 'Now Mr Sham Lal will give a speech.' Sham Lal slowly shuffled to his feet, cleared his throat, and, as the packed hall waited in anticipation for an outpouring of enlightenment from the man who had attained intellectual nirvana, he merely said, 'Thank you'. Then he went back to his chair and sat down.

Sham Lal wrote a weekly column, Life And Letters, under the pen-name Adib in the exalted space of the edit page special (the '3,4,5'as it was called, referring to the columns of the traditional 8-col paper). It was meant to be a review article, but it always ended up presenting Sham Lal's own world view. The subjects were esoteric, the treatment an intellectual analysis: French existentialists, German epistology, dissidents in communist regimes, Polish plays. It was sardonic, caustic, contemptuous of anything philistine. It was also a great showcase of the pliancy of the English language in the hands of a master, and it had a small but absolutely devoted following.

Sham Lal was a socialist, but never a Marxist. In fact he shut down *Times Weekly*, so successfully edited by Darry D'Monte, because he felt it was veering too much to the Left. Of course, the closure could have been nudged by the two government directors who were for some years on the board of Bennett. The Jains got back full control of the company in 1978.

The paper not standing up against the Emergency-unlike RP Goenka's *Indian Express* and

CR Irani's *Statesman* – could also have been on account of the presence of the two government appointees on the board, but Sham Lal came under a lot of flak after the draconian declaration was lifted in 1977. He was not pro-Mrs Gandhi, but Girilal Jain, then the RE in Delhi, decidedly was.

LEGENDS OF SHAM LAL

Gautam Adhikari was only one of the many young assistant editors who came under his thrall, "Sham Lal, the acclaimed intellectual, and I, the aspiring intellectual. After he moved to Delhi, when he invited you for a drink at his house, he would hand you the weakest whiskey you could imagine, but the conversation would fire the belly. Sometimes his paying guest, Ian Jack, the India correspondent of London's *Sunday Times*, would join us."

When he visited Mumbai after he retired, he would politely call Gautam to ask, "What are you doing? Would you like to go for a walk?" They would stroll up to Churchgate and have coffee in the open-air section of Gaylord's. Once they just strolled on Marine Drive, bought peanuts and sat on the parapet talking till it got dark. Gautam added, "Sham Lal never liked gossip. But Giri loved it."

At a party in Mumbai, Sham Lal was cornered by a large, garrulous American woman. After a 15-minute monologue, she stopped mid-flow and asked, "Am I boring you?" and Sham Lal replied with extreme and genuine courtesy, "Yes I am afraid you are."

Yet he had all the time in the world for people who aspired to an intellectual plane, however low they might be on the popularity scale (in any case most intellectuals fell into that category, and would be deeply mortified if they did not.)

Bakr Mehdi was an Urdu poet whose books never sold more than 23 copies, but the legendary editor was completely at ease with him and spent hours in his company.

Nanporia's was an outstanding mind and he was a brilliant writer, as much about Ming pottery as about political mandarins of every ilk in every period.

50% PARSI, 50% JAPANESE, 100% INTELLECTUAL

This is a story about NJ Nanporia, but it has been told about virtually every introvert editor in every part of the world. In one of his rare forays into Mumbai's cocktail circuit, a man struck up a conversation with him. Nanporia was diffident, but the chap was not to be shaken off. The editor was also intrigued by his interests. The interlocutor wanted to know the esoteric differences between China and Japan, subjects which NJN was extremely knowledgeable about, indeed he wrote of the entire 'Far East' with passion. So he asked the man what he did for a living, and got the embarrassing reply, "Sir I'm your News Editor."

The diminutive, elfin Nanporia was that exotic hybrid of Parsi and Japanese, and his Sunday pastime was the scouring of Chor Bazar. His was an outstanding mind and he too was a brilliant writer, as much about Ming pottery as about political mandarins of every ilk in every period.

50% PARSI, 50% JAPANESE, 100% INTELLECTUAL

Like his predecessor Frank Moraes, Nanporia's 'writing' style was remarkable. Both paced up and down their spacious rooms dictating to their stenos, right down to punctuation marks. Frank's PA would take it down in shorthand; Nanporia's would do so directly on his typewriter, khut-khut-khut. It was an unending marvel how unhesitatingly flowed the stream of perfectly framed sentences and perfectly turned phrases.

It was even more amazing that they knew exactly when to stop. They dictated exactly the right number of words needed for an edit or a '3-4-5', the prestigious special article at the top of the Edit Page. Both Moraes and Nanporia would cast a glance over the steno's offering, but they did no editing and their copy never needed to be cut. Nor would anyone dare to.

Most of them [assistant editors] were from Oxbridge as was the tradition across the English-language print media, and print was the only media.

THE BRAINS TRUST

The Old Lady of Bori Bunder stood at the head of the heritage mile of D.N. Road, flanked by the similarly Indo-Saracenic Municipal Corporation headquarters. Even the Gothic Victoria Terminus across the road deferred to this dowager empress. A concourse of people, however multitudinous or grand, is no match for a concourse of ideas.

The nerve centre was The Editorial Conference which shaped the TOI edit page. In the 1970s and '80s, apart from the presiding editor, it comprised such veterans as Inder Malhotra, KC Khanna, AS Abraham, MV Mathew and Prem Shankar Jha as well as Rahul Singh, Darryl D'Monte, Gautam Adhikari, Gautam SG Vohra and Achin Vanaik. Most of them were from Oxbridge as was the tradition across the English-language print media, and print was the only media.

In those days, editorial conferences in all newspaper offices had the quality of higher liturgy. They were held in the paper's sanctum sanctorum, the editor's office, and if you didn't actually hear a Gregorian chant, you were certainly expected to hear the crash of falling governments. Assistant editors jealously guarded their stature as Masters of the Universe. Even if they were doodling or making weekend plans, it would be heresy to think they were doing anything other than stewarding the State. In all mythology, assumption triumphs over reality.

THE BRAINS TRUST

Significantly, Laxman refused to budge when the editorial and management HQ was shifted to Delhi in the late 1980s. He rightly believed that his vital objectivity would melt if it came too physically close to the political sun.

The daily conclave had a set ritual, sanctified by decades of tradition. Each incumbent of the chair brought his own shades of solemnity – and quirkiness. The male pronoun is specifically used; 'He' does not encompass 'she' as in constitutional or legal parlance. Till recently, editors were men, and the Star Chamber was an entirely male club, with all its attendant grand-standing. Fatma Zakaria broke the TOI's gender barrier in Girilal Jain's time.

Fatma Zakaria broke the TOI's gender barrier in Girilal Jain's time.

In the reign of Giri, the editorial conference become more regal than it had been during the tenure of the professorial Sham Lal. It began sharp at 10 am, and all the assistant editors were expected to be ready and waiting in their ribbed-glass cabins for the 'summons'. These were delivered by Bhagwati, Giri's wiry peon with a droopy moustache and a twinkling eye. He would come to each, and announce, 'Chai taiyar hai.'

(At the more feudal Calcutta *Statesman*, peons were referred to as 'piyadas' and Bhagwati's counterpart would push open the heavier Burma teak doors to proclaim 'Sah'b ne salaam bheja.' The Sah'b was certainly not sending polite greetings; this was the euphemism for an order to present yourself on the double. On my first day there in 1980, I had looked askance and mumbled, 'Sah'b ko wapas salaam de dijiya.' Ram Pershad-ji almost passed out at such insolence, that too from a woman who had defiled the male sanctity of assistant editorship.)

The chai at the edit conference wasn't some plebian 'taiyar' variety. And it certainly wasn't Mumbai's patented half-a-glass 'cutting chai'. It came in a proper fine china tea service.

The chai at the edit conference wasn't some plebian 'taiyar' variety. And it certainly wasn't Mumbai's patented half-a-glass 'cutting chai'. It came in a proper fine china tea service.

The meeting would start with pleasantries, then Giri would say something profound on the state of the world, lighting his pipe and staring into the great beyond. This would be followed by grand disputes (largely one-sided) over such esoteric matters as the Hindu mind and the idea of India. Giri didn't really care for anything south of the Vindhyas. For him the nation had to be defined from one powerful centre which had to hold it together.

The assistant editors were arranged around the editor's large desk. AS Abraham was the seniormost in the Mumbai team till Kumud Khanna arrived, so he sat in the centre, with Achin Vanaik, Gautam Vohra, Praful Bidwai and Fatma Zakaria fanning out from either side. Sometimes, Prem Shankar Jha or Inder Malhotra, visiting from Delhi, would be present, both hyperventilating as was their style.

Laxman, by virtue of his elevated position in the hierarchy, sat at the outer edge of this mystic semi-circle, and Gautam Adhikari, then the newest member of the elite club, was consigned to the other end. Because Laxman was out of Giri's line of sight, and more so because he was

Laxman, he would sit through all this, pulling faces and imitating the editor as he puffed on his pipe and made his ex cathedra pronouncements. He would do this catching the eye of Gautam, who would find it impossible not to crack up, let alone concentrate on the complex theories being expounded.

THE BRAINS TRUST

The last 15 minutes of the hour long edit conference were devoted to the actual purpose. Edits were apportioned, and you were expected to finish them before lunch. That was Giri's diktat. Abe and Achin wrote by hand, most of the others typed theirs out. The edits would then go to either of Giri's two PAs, more powerful than the others of their ilk, because they were the gatekeepers to the holy of holies. They would space them out correctly, tote the word count (this was before 'Tools'), hand them back to the respective assistant editors for any needed cutting, and then the edits would be borne in to Giri.

Giri usually called for a tray from the Directors Lunch Room, and ate in his cabin in the company of Fatma and perhaps Laxman. Sometimes, his astrologer would drop in. High-rise intellectuals are not necessarily rationalists. Then the lights in his cabin would be switched off, and he would take a 30-minute nap on the couch.

Refreshed, or rather charged up, he would attack the edits. Sometimes they emerged largely unscathed, at other times he would slash and burn, and entirely rewrite. If the subject was Mrs Gandhi or a momentous national issue, it would have his stamp all over.

By 3.30 pm, the final edits were ready, but the assistant editors couldn't just skedaddle off. For the next two hours, they were expected to remain in office, expanding and enriching their minds with books, newspapers, magazines – or discussion (aka gossip). They would leave at 5.30 pm sharp, an impossible luxury in later, more frenetic, times.

Gautam Adhikari would always be first off the block so that he could catch the train to Bandra on the Harbour Line from VT across the road. Once he was collared by SP Singh, who later became editor of *Navbharat Times*. "Why are you always rushing off?" he demanded with his usual cynical smile. Gautam replied, "Because I have to catch the 5.57."

"Look, both of us [Gautam Adhikari and SP Singh] come from Calcutta. We don't understand this '5.57' business. For us, it is chhey bajey ke aas paas. It's 6-ish. Tumhari train chhodo, yaar, let's go for a drink to Press Club instead."

SP gave him a bemused, almost pitying, look and said, "Look, both of us come from Calcutta. We don't understand this '5.57' business. For us, it is chhey bajey ke aas paas. It's 6-ish. Tumhari train chhodo, yaar, let's go for a drink to Press Club instead." Of course they did.

In the post-Giri era, the edit page was made into an independent entity, headed by an edit page editor who did not report to the executive editor. The logic was that comment had to be distanced from the way news was given play. We will meet this new edit page later in the time of Jug Suraiya.

FROM TOI, WITH PREM

Prem Shankar Jha, a large,
balding teddy bear of a man,
was the most blustery and disorganized of the TOI's
assistant editors in the 1970s.
His daily arrival was as unorthodox.

The editorial HQ was still Mumbai, and he wouldn't roll up to the portico in a taxi like his colleagues. He arrived with his bulk perched incongruously on a frail moped. He would come directly from his morning tennis at the Bombay Gym and would fluster into the edit meeting, invariably late, dripping with sweat and clumsily dropping his helmet and racquet. Sham Lal would mildly glower, and Prem would clasp his podgy hands and say, 'Maaf kijiye, Sham Lalji, maaf kijiye". The other-wordly editor, not quite knowing how to handle this man, would just get on with the meeting.

Prem was constantly losing his handwritten edit. He would rant and rave, then quieten down and rewrite it in 20 minutes flat. He would give it to his steno, Iyer, to type and retype because he would keep making furious corrections. Computers would come in only at the end of the '80s with due initial rejection by the intellectuals who had grudgingly accepted the typewriter as a necessary evil; some had held out, insisting that only the fountain pen was the ordained instrument to transfer thought to paper. Jug is the last man standing who still does.

FROM TOI, WITH PREM

One day, hearing hysterical screams from the inner cabin, the long-suffering Iyer entered to find his portly boss balanced precariously on a chair, quaking in impotent terror and staring at a cockroach on his desk. As soon as he saw his steno, he ordered him to swat it. Iyer froze at such an unBrahminical directive, with Prem getting more and more apoplectic by the minute. He finally shouted, "Kill it, kill it, you f___ing vegetarian." Iyer fled.

Computers would come in only at the end of the '80s with due initial rejection by the intellectuals who had grudgingly accepted the typewriter as a necessary evil.

Prem was always rambunctious, vocally passionate on whatever seized his mind at the moment. He would burst into the edit meeting, and bulldoze over any conversation that had been in progress. For instance, a serious discussion on the merits and nuances of the Vietnam war had been on since the start of the meeting a good 15 minutes earlier when Prem arrived frothing in rage and saying, "Sham Lalji, we have to do an edit on all the garbage that is thrown into the Arabian sea." You must remember that in those days the lofty cabal never deigned to consider the journalistic axiom that 'the dead dog in the street outside is more important than a flood in China'. They would have been appalled at such an absurd suggestion.

Prem naturally did not confine these burst-ins and outbursts to the office. He and his lovely dancer wife were a sociable couple, but while the soft-spoken and graceful Usha was like a leaf in a lily pool, Prem was the cosmic churning of the ocean itself. And spewing poison too.

If he overheard a snatch of conversation that he didn't agree with it, he would leave his group, stride over and join issue with the hapless, and stunned, maker of the remark. He would then proceed to hijack the conversation, and do so in tones so loud and belligerent, that the rest of the party had no choice but to stop its talk and listen captively. But, to be fair, not unwillingly. For Prem most often had something more substantial and thought-triggering to say than the standard party chitter-chatter.

He [Prem Shankar Jha] and his lovely dancer wife were a sociable couple, but while the soft-spoken and graceful Usha was like a leaf in a lily pool, Prem was the cosmic churning of the ocean itself. And spewing poison too.

Apart from Prem there was another Jha in the organization, Surendra, editor of *Science Today*. They were in some quarters distinguished as Fat Ass Jha and Just Jha, respectively.

M & M

"If you've written it,
put it into this tray.
If you haven't,
go home and write it."

Other characters of the '70s 'Editorial Corridor' in Mumbai were Muthanna and Mathew. Muthanna always wore fawn-coloured suede shoes and had the light eyes, martial bearing and twirled moustaches of his Coorgi community. He was once travelling to Pune in a coupe. His co-passenger entered, extended a friendly hand, and said, "Good-morning, I'm Khanna." "I'm not," replied Muthanna, without even glancing up from his book.

Equally taciturn – and brilliant – was MV Mathew – who used to write third edits, and handle Middles and Letters to the Editor. In those 'Security-free' times, the letter writers would walk into his cabin and start elaborating on their point of view. Mathew would give them a scornful look, and say through his teeth, "If you've written it, put it into this tray. If you haven't, go home and write it."

He was TOI's English theatre critic, and his acerbic reviews comprised such gentle lines as "The director should be tied to a post and publicly flogged for inflicting such an abysmal play on the audience."

Mathew's real forte, however, was science, and he wrote with awesome lucidity on its complexities. Sham Lal was least excited by the subject but deferred to Mathew's passion. The assistant editor would return to his cabin after the morning meeting, smoke a Charminar (yes you could do that in the office till the late 1980s) and then write out a perfectly crafted edit in one hour. He was the only assistant editor whose copy didn't require the changing of even a single comma.

OLIVETTIS & OLIVES

He [Ashok Thapar] was torn between the Old Lady of Bori Bunder and the New Lady of Barcelona.

Ashok Thapar, another assistant editor from the Gilded Age, didn't last on the job or the profession as long as the greats. He used to write on agriculture and got a scholarship to Oxford. There he met a Spanish girl, one of the 'language school hotties'. They were both lonely, and fell in love. He was torn between the Old Lady of Bori Bunder and the New Lady of Barcelona. "I want to keep working in a newspaper," he told her, looking into her waiting Spanish eyes. She turned to her father for advice. Rich Papa said, "I'll buy one for him." Thapar was last heard of looking after the senor's acres of olive groves.

SHOOT-OUT AT B ZAFAR MARG

'Why don't they have a Wild West kind of shoot-out – after all the guns are there – and settle their differences once and for all?'

The incumbent Girilal Jain and the newly inducted Arun Shourie were at daggers drawn from the moment the latter stepped into the TOI's Delhi office. This was at the height of the Punjab problem, and both used to write at length and strongly against the terror unleashed by the Khalistani militants. So they both had personal security guards. The joke doing the rounds was, 'Why don't they have a Wild West kind of shoot-out – after all the guns are there – and settle their differences once and for all?'

Fatma was not a writer
but she could certainly put together
a star-studded magazine
or edit page.

'Z' CATEGORY

The first woman assistant editor at the *Times of India* was the stunning Fatma Zakaria. She did not have the cerebral power of her male colleagues, but she drew on the political circle of her husband, Dr Rafiq Zakaria, a cabinet minister in the Maharashtra government, a Nehruvian acolyte, an acclaimed historian and an affirmed secularist.

Fatma's connections – and her own manifest organisational abilities –first pitchforked her to editorial importance, right below Khushwant Singh, who had soon realized that she was wasting her time as the Aunty Wendy of the *Illustrated Weekly of India*'s children's page.

After Khushwant Singh's fall from grace, Fatma came one floor down to the TOI of Girilal Jain. He was, if anything, more impressed by Fatma's capabilities and social graces. Fatma was not a writer but she could certainly put together a star-studded magazine or edit page. With the downfall of Giri in 1989, she left the TOI Group, and took her talents to the Taj Magazine.

Ashok Jain summoned Gautam, and said, "I am told there are no good young journalists in India outside the Times."

PARLEZ-VOUS DILEEP

Some time in 1987, Ashok Jain summoned Gautam, and said, "I am told there are no good young journalists in India outside the Times." The comment is believed to have been prompted by Giri's foot-dragging over the changes that the raring Samir had wanted to put in place. Giri had also wanted Fatma Zakaria to be made resident editor of the flagship Mumbai edition, a desire not embraced with any degree of enthusiasm on either side of the 3rd floor landing.

Gautam, said, "No, sir, there are many good journalists, and I am sure they would be happy to join us." The Chairman said, "Give me a note." Gautam made out a spreadsheet which included their brief bios, even a ballpark estimate of their current salaries. Not surprisingly it had an overwhelming Kolkata contingent. This was not for parochial reasons, but because it was the country's most cerebral city, and, *The Statesman* especially still bred journalists and writers honed in the best professional standards.

This legendary paper, however, was already in rapid decline. Gautam's list included Chandan Mitra, Swapan Dasgupta and Jug Suraiya from there. Shekhar Bhatia from *The Telegraph* was also on it, but he refused at the time. He would come as executive editor of the TOI at the turn of the millennium.

Suddenly, there was this buzz in the media world, 'Have you been approached?'

Swapan and Chandan were political animals to the core, so no one doubted that they would jump at the chance to move to the capital and the much more influential TOI. Swapan, in fact, was already with the Delhi edition of *The Statesman*. Jug, however, was part of the woodwork of *The Statesman*, and it seemed equally impossible that he could survive outside Calcutta's rarefied ambience.

Suddenly, there was this buzz in the media world, 'Have you been approached?'

When Gautam called his old quizzing friend, and said, "Could we meet?" Jug thought he wanted to join *The Statesman*, and sounded out the editor. Sunanda Datta-Ray removed his cigarette-holder from his lips and replied, "He will be an asset. Ask him to telephone me." But when they met at the Elphin Bar, it was Gautam who was doing the offering. To everyone's surprise, Suraiya was willing.

"But where will I stay?" he suddenly asked, thinking of his huge, old flat on Wood Street so conveniently located exactly opposite his Saturday Club. "Ass Eds get houses in Delhi. You can look for one. The allowance is good enough," was Gautam's response.

PARLEZ-VOUS DILEEP

Jug got excited, and they both got so carried away that they carried themselves right out of the door – without paying the bill. It's still outstanding. Chandan said "I do" over a jug of beer at The Other Room, near Trinca's on Park Street. Swapan would be approached a year later.

Then there was the matter of Dileep Padgaonkar being sniffed out as a possible successor to Giri. He had worked earlier at the TOI, he was Sorbonne-educated, cosmopolitan and had all the accoutrements needed to take the TOI out of its Old Lady image.

He was then at UNESCO, and his boss, Mbow, was bowing out, so perhaps he did not want to start establishing himself with the new incumbent. Gautam was going to New York with the director, Ramesh Chandra, to explore the possibility of taking over the diaspora paper, *India Abroad*. The Jains decided that the duo should stop in Paris to see if Dileep was indeed their man.

It was Gautam's first visit to Europe. He reached a day earlier than Ramesh-ji. Landing at night at the airport, he asked for a hotel, took the Metro as directed and landed up in the flesh-pot of the Pigalle. The commended hostelry was really seedy, and the only local number he had was Dileep's. He waited sleeplessly and in a state of consternation over the comings and goings through the night. Then, at the reasonable hour of 7 am, he called, and explained his predicament.

He [Dileep Padgaonkar] had worked earlier at the TOI, he was Sorbonne-educated, cosmopolitan and had all the accoutrements needed to take the TOI out of its Old Lady image.

"Oh, I understand," said the suave voice at the other end. "Take the Metro to Duplex station and I'll meet you there." Gautam got off as instructed and walked down the length of the still-deserted platform, suitcase in hand. Then he saw a figure emerge from the mist and come towards him. It was a scene straight out of a Truffaut film.

PARLEZ-VOUS DILEEP

Dileep took Gautam to the definitely more respectable Hotel Tourisme, and introduced him to a nearby café where they sat over kir talking of international politics, old Hindi songs and the qualities of French women. Thus began a long friendship.

Ramesh-ji arrived the following day, and he of course had a booking at a fancy hotel near the Champs D'Elysees.They took him to the same café. The strict Jain perused the menu with increasing discomfiture, and said, "Yeh jambon kya hai? Woh hi manga lo." Dileep discreetly said, "Ji nahin, yeh jamun jaisi cheez nahin hain. Why don't you order a salad?"

"I don't eat cheese or onion and garlic," was the difficult reply. Even a croissant was out of the question because it had egg. In Parisian French, Dileep asked the garcon to *s'il vous plait* whip up something circumventing all these dietary hurdles. The man came back disdainfully bearing a dish which met with no one else's approval either.

Padgaonkar was offered the job of Foreign Editor. Hair-splitters might murmur about influencing the jury, but since both parties were equally interested in each other anyway, who cared?

So Dileep offered, "Why don't you come home this evening? My wife will cook you a pure vegetarian and delicious Saraswat meal." Latika did. And lunch the next day too. The 'interviews' were conducted over these repasts. And the future was assured. Padgaonkar was offered the job of Foreign Editor. Hair-splitters might murmur about influencing the jury, but since both parties were equally interested in each other anyway, who cared?

It would be a successful corporate enterprise catering for, and creating, the aspiring and empowered 'right kind of reader' who would attract the 'right kind of advertiser'.

BOTOX FOR THE BROADSHEET

The Calcutta Conclave of July '87 was a tipping point. It was the bolder equivalent of the economic reforms process which would hit India in the solar plexus five years later. At this meeting were laid out the Botox, the implants, the makeover instruments which would turn the Old Lady of Bori Bunder into a smart, post-national babe, as adept at breaking media glass ceilings as swirling a goblet of Beaujolais.

It would no longer be the Times of ivy-smothered intellectuals in ivory towers. It would be a successful corporate enterprise catering for, and creating, the aspiring and empowered 'right kind of reader' who would attract the 'right kind of advertiser'. For the next decade, there would be no God but Samir Jain, and Pradeep Guha was his Profit. The editor would be the more conventional prophet.

Dr Ram Tarneja was still the MD, and Samir was the JMD, but he was the heir apparent, and made it very apparent. He had made up his mind that Dileep would be the next editor. What loaded the dice in Padgaonkar's favour were his international exposure and his personal style with a wife to match. The TOI was to move from a statist to a global view, and its editor had to be a citizen of the world.

By then Arun Shourie had quit; he was clearly not cut out to be what the TOI wanted to be. For obvious reasons, Samir did not share his plans with Giri; the idea was to let him continue while the successor got a three-year grooming.

The Calcutta Conclave wasn't held only in meeting rooms. Setting a style that would become a Samir patent, it included long, discursive walks on the lawns of the Jain mansion in Alipore. This was the city's 'millionaire mile', bejewelled with other stately homes belonging to the Marwaris who had taken over the English and Scots managing agencies and empires of jute, tea and coal. Gautam recalled that exotic fruit was always on the table, and it was the first time that he encountered nectarines.

The TOI was to move from a statist to a global view, and its editor had to be a citizen of the world.

Dileep's three-year grooming was cut to one for several reasons. He had been Giri's staunch ally in his battle with Shourie, but when Dileep's candidate Darryl D'Monte was appointed RE of the Mumbai edition over Giri's choice of Fatma Zakaria, the rift between the two began. In any event, the organisation was heading for the great churning which would be set in motion as the TOI entered its 150th year. It was a historic milestone. More so because history was about to be junked.

When Padgaonkar was officially appointed editor in 1988, he called Gautam, who had by then moved to the US, and said, "Guv, it's done."

BOTOX FOR THE BROADSHEET

Why 'Guv?' Ever since Gautam's rescue from the seductions of the Pigalle, their friendship had blossomed. It bloomed when the two of them lived together for six months like one family in two adjacent rooms with their wives in the Jains' Lutyens bungalow on Delhi's 4, Tilak Marg. They were both great entertainers, and had once done a skit from 'My Fair Lady' for their own amusement. Gautam had played the Cockney Mr Doolittle, and Dileep had called him 'Guv' ever since.

Darryl's appointment was part of the master plan to manifest change, and he would get a sharp new inner circle of senior editors, the new designation for the elite corps of assistant editors. Many of them had been drawn back to the new dawn so clearly breaking over the tired organisation they had once loved but had chosen to jilt. Darryl himself had left TOI to join the *Indian Express* and then work on his own.

The fine-boned and finer-minded Shanta Gokhale, formerly of Femina, and this chronicler, formerly of the *Illustrated Weekly*, were also former groupies. From the outside came Kalpana Sharma, an authority on the Seven Sisters of the Northeast and developmental issues. She joined from the Express; Rajdeep Sardesai arrived fresh from Oxford.

Darryl had invited us all for lunch to his seaside, family bungalow on Mumbai's Carter Road. This would be an opportunity for us to meet Samir Jain and get an idea of the TOI he wanted us to shape. Till then we knew of our future colleagues only as rumour, or not even that. No one was really sure who was ditching their old papers for the lure of the brave new TOI. So as each person entered the door, a collective gasp and a silent 'Et tu, Brute' shimmied through the spacious drawing room.

Darryl's appointment was part of the master plan for manifest change, and he would get a sharp new inner circle of senior editors, the new designation for the elite corps of assistant editors.

At one point Darryl's teenaged son passed by where this writer sat with Samir Jain. She blithely said, "Sameer, meet Samir." Mr Jain chatted with the boy. It was only after several months in BCCL when she came to know of his fastidiousness about correct behaviour, that she realized how incorrectly she had crossed the line. She continues to be mortified by the memory.

MANY A SLIP

Sometimes a 'mistake' is a mistaken one.

The Big Cheeses of the Edit Page could be a bit mouldy. One of them wrote an entire 3rd edit speaking of the dolphin as though it were a bird. It was saved.

An executive editor of the past wrote a signed Page 1 piece using the phrase 'short & curly'. Even in its correct form, 'short and curlies,' it would have raised eyebrows in those less-liberal days. Literally, it refers to a rather private patch of the human body.

Not quite in the same league, but scandalising none the less was the expression used by K.K. Dua, this one too in a front-page, signed editorial. Condemning the Rs 950-crore fodder scam that came to light in 1996, the editor wrote about Lalu 'fondling the udders of cows'.

Sometimes a 'mistake' is a mistaken one.

In 1997, Siddharth Varadarajan had returned from a UK trip. This was the time when the VC happened to be in a distinctly anti-British mood, branding it as a 'Third World country'. He convinced Sid, who wrote a piece called 'Rue Britannia'. He soon got a call from Joel Lyall on the

Delhi newsdesk, who sounded as pleased as Punch. "Sir, sir," said the over-enthusiastic sub, "Hamney toh aap ko bacha diya. I have really spared you major embarrassment. The spelling you used of Britannia is that of the biscootwala (Britannia biscuits)." There's actually no such difference.

In the '70s, the *Times Weekly* was the earlier avatar of the *Sunday Times of India*. It did so well, that it was even sold separately. Darryl D'Monte was in charge, and someone had written a piece on the list of top income-tax payers, and why certain industrialists did not figure. One of his assistants was the prim Cecilia D'Souza (whom the younger women of another department had wickedly nicknamed 'five feet above sea level' because her petticoat hem was always substantially higher than that of her nylon sari).

Cecilia had, in her wisdom, randomly illustrated the article with photographs of JRD Tata and G.D. Birla. Prem Jha, in his usual blustery fashion, stormed into the cabin of Sham Lal, and ranted, "They'll sue the paper!" And Sham Lal, unable to imagine that such an outrage could be committed in the TOI, asked mildly, "In which edition of Blitz did it appear?" An apology was painstakingly drafted and printed the following Sunday.

***

There is a big bogey in every newspaper and he is called the Printer's Devil.

Zubin Mehta's visits to Mumbai with an accompanying symphony orchestra always make for big media events. In March 2003, *The Times of India* did its usual curtain raiser that appeared on the morning of the concert. The piece was suitably worshipful of the maestro, except for the havoc wreaked by a rogue spell check that had replaced philharmonic with philanthropic. All through the piece, in four places. Zubin Mehta himself was quoted as saying, "The first time I

There is a big bogey in every newspaper and he is called the Printer's Devil.

heard the Vienna Philanthrophic was at the Vienna Opera House." That evening, when the editor and correspondent went to the performance at the NCPA, they didn't budge from their seats during the wine-and-sandwich break for fear of being accosted by old Parsis berating them for falling standards.

MANY A SLIP

Khushwant Singh's (predictable) favourite was the headline 'Pen Is Mightier Than The Sword' appearing without a space between the first two words.

'Public' is a more common minefield, the big fear being that it will appear without the crucial 'l'. This must have occurred on several occasions at the Times, but let us record the time it happened on the watch of the hapless Cecilia. To make matters worse, the sin of omission again took place throughout an article on the Union Public Service Commission.

"The Times gives you such huge reputations, you should be paying the company instead."

PAY LOAD

CR Irani at the Statesman kept journalists on the verge of penury because he believed that paying them well would make them fat and complacent; hunger instead would stoke the fire in their belly. In BCCL, editors are now far better paid – some even pampered.

But for a long time the belief persisted that journalists get their rewards, aka lionising, from the outside world, and the management has done enough merely by providing them this enviable platform. The GM of the '70s, PR Krishnamurthy said so, in so many words, "The Times gives you such huge reputations, you should be paying the company instead."

PAS, PEONS & OTHER WORTHIES

The Doberwoman in the outer cabin is, after all, the hound guarding access to the Almighty.

As in most great institutions, secretaries often end up being more formidable than the boss; the Doberwoman in the outer cabin is, after all, the hound guarding access to the Almighty. The TOI has had its legendary stenos, all of them male, right up to around the '70s, and usually part of the 'Mal-net', the Malayali network.

TR Mannikan drew his proxy stature from his powerful boss, the omnipotent GM of the 1970s, Dr Ram S Tarneja. Mannikan was one of those bustling busybodies, always ready to prove how he was your man if you needed anything fixed or speeded. The solicitousness was often an ally for his snooping. He was his boss's eyes and ears, even when Dr T did not want the extra pairs.

A young journalist at the Weekly travelling to the UK on a three-month course at Cardiff, Wales, had been helped by a senior colleague with connections in the travel trade to go on an Air France ticket which would give her a decent sum of cash at her destination. This was extremely helpful in the time of the absurd forex allowance of $20.

How or why Mannikan got into the picture, no one quite fathomed, but he sweet-talked the young woman till she blurted out the arrangement. It made no difference to anyone, but Mannikan just had to know why the ticket hadn't been routed through him, and the poor girl felt like she had embezzled the company's coffers.

The GM's office was almost the seal of God in those days; it not only sanctioned trips, but did all the bookings.

The GM's office was almost the seal of God in those days; it not only sanctioned trips, but did all the bookings. With all his official and creative experience, Mannikan managed a post-retirement deal by which he continued to do the ticketing for all business travel by group employees.

On the editorial side, the PAs also orchestrated the exchange of edits and news lists between the two main publishing centres of Mumbai and Delhi, apart from keeping the grapevine loaded with everything that was happening in their migrant lives.

Through the '90s and beyond, 'Shesh' in TOI B and 'Krish' in TOI D were in almost hourly communication, but never once met in person. Their efficiency, like that of their colleagues Shankar Narayanan and Shivdas, both in Mumbai editorial, was legendary. Arguably, the edition would not have appeared the next morn if they hadn't been there to knit together all the bits and pieces.

Sheshanand had the keys to Giri's kingdom, and when the editor was away in Delhi, Praful Bidwai, Achin Vanaik and several of the other younger assistant editors would take turns to go have an afternoon catnap in the editor's hallowed cabin

Unnikrishnan, 'Unni', was among the true 'characters', driving many an editor to despair with his self-importance. When he was assigned to her, a senior editor and columnist handling the *Sunday Times* told him, "Unni, please remember, I am very particular about my clippings being properly filed." And Unni replied without blinking, "I am also particular about my clippings."

PAS, PEONS & OTHER WORTHIES

He did have clippings. With the assistance of Kalpana Sharma, Unni had written some news reports. He stayed in the faraway suburb of Dombivli where reporters didn't venture, and certainly not at the time when an eponymous fever raged through it, necessitating TOI attention.

He accused the same boss of discrimination for asking him not to smoke in the office. He muttered darkly to one of the subs, "She doesn't complain when Jerry Pinto puffs away," adding, "I also need a cigarette when I'm brainstorming." Indeed.

Why just the stenos, even the peons were totally clued in and, when it came to Byzantine state politics, the Maharashtrian ones could teach a thing or two to the younger assistant editors. Once Rajdeep Sardesai, hot off the dreaming spires of Oxford, wrote a whole three-part series on the rising presence of the Shiv Sena without, it was whispered, meeting a single sainik or visiting a single shakha.

On that occasion, it was left to the more hands-on Kalpana Sharma to fill in the gaps. But on another, Shinde, the peon, spotted a factual error in an edit while reading it as he took the copy up to the page make-up room, and prevented embarrassment.

When fair-minded members of the editorial team suggested that Shinde be given a monetary reward for his vigilance, the same GM, P.R. Krishnamurthy, 'correctly' bristled. "On the contrary, the fellow should be penalised for acting outside his designated duties," he reportedly said.

During the grand sesquicentennial celebrations, the heritage building received an internal makeover to the grand design of Hafeez Contractor. The newly re-christened Response department got granite floors, Rajasthani jharokas, expensive art – and a tall, polyurethane potted palm. It took weeks to convince one particular peon that he should stop watering it religiously every day.

And speaking of religion, two stories:

A long-timer was Nair, who was a favourite because he was the peon who encashed the conveyance vouchers which could be filled in for writing Citylights items. When he retired, a generous collection gave him a tea party in the newsroom and a fancy wall clock. He was overcome with emotion, but through his tears he said that no one should ever come and meet him in his native village.

A long-timer was Nair, who was a favourite because he was the peon who encashed the conveyance vouchers which could be filled in for writing Citylights items.

Everyone assumed this was because he might be ashamed of his modest circumstances, but a busybody made it his business to find out why Nair was so adamant. On his next trip home to his own nearby village, he made a detour. And discovered that Nair in fact was Muslim, and through all those decades in Mumbai, he had successfully camouflaged his religious identity.

Those were still the days of hot-metal typesetting. Every year, at Dussehra time, a retired press hand would come with a basketful of marigolds to garland the linotype machines. No one paid much attention to an old-timer staggering out with a tokri still topped with leftover flowers. Till one day he tripped, and out fell a heap of lead bars. Proving that you can serve both God and Mammon, he had been regularly smuggling out this expensive material on the pretext of performing puja.

And talking of pilfering, all kinds of material was spirited away in the days when the TOI ran like a government department – because it was in the control of the government. Even more surreal is this story. Piece by piece, an entire linotype-setting machine was stolen. The theft was discovered only when the enterprising fellow set up shop with the reassembled whole, and took on job work.

PAS, PEONS & OTHER WORTHIES

In dishonesty, caste, creed or category is no bar. A senior HR man would park his car some distance from the others lined up in the lanes of the municipal corporation and the Anjuman-i-Islam building which flanked the TOI to left and right. It was later discovered that every evening, a sack of onions and potatoes from the canteen was surreptitiously loaded into his boot to service his own kitchen, and probably that of his extended family.

SHARMAJI

KK Sharma...finally acquired a car... he would...tether it to the trunk of a tree with a bicycle chain. "Whom can you trust? The car is mine. Only I have to take care of its safety."

KK Sharma was chief sub on the Delhi Desk. When he finally acquired a car, he would drive it cautiously to office, and tether it to the trunk of a tree with a bicycle chain. When it was pointed out, "But, Sharmaji, there are parking attendants," he would retort, "Whom can you trust? The car is mine. Only I have to take care of its safety."

To be fair he took as much care of his office responsibilities as he did of his car. In those '90s, the bromides would be glued to the layout sheets by the 'paste-up men' in the make-up room which was one floor below the newsroom.

TIMES HOUSE

Those hastily making the pages every night were in the habit of just snipping off the galleys where the page ended, regardless of whether the sentence did, let alone the paragraph. So, often, the paste-up guys and even the subs would have to go down on all fours to look for words or even letters among the scissored bits of bromides scattered on the floor. These would have to be individually pasted to complete the mindlessly amputated sentence.

SHARMAJI

Then Sharmaji would descend the spiral staircase from the newsroom for the coup de grace of the final check and signing off. He did so in a signature style. He would read every headline aloud, syllable by syllable, 'Del-hi Un-der Po-lice Con-t-rol.'

***

Linotype operators of yore were a breed unto themselves. They could read the text simply by running their finger down the lines. Blocks of copy would be 'set' on the stone, 'locked', and transported as a page of metal paragraphs. A printer's worst nightmare was someone dropping it, and the metals lines lying in a collapsed mess on the setting-room floor with seconds to go to the deadline. It happened seldom, but happen it did.

CROSS WORDS

"Darryl, my boy,
you have created
a serious problem.
I'm now bloody constipated.
I used to do the crossword
every morning
in the bathroom.
And without it I can't go."

The newsprint shortage of the '70s led to two casualties, the crossword and the astrology forecast from Sunday's *Times Weekly*. Both triggered loud howls of protest and cancelled subscriptions. There was as much internal revolt. VS Thirumalai, the Advertising Manager, loped into Darryl D'Monte's room, and said in his peculiar accent, "Darryl, my boy, you have created a serious problem. I'm now bloody constipated. I used to do the crossword every morning in the bathroom. And without it I can't go." Darryl replied, "Maybe you should call it 'Moving with the Times'."

Darryl had used the shortage to axe the astrology section because it went against his own rationalist grain. When he was confronted by angry readers, he would say, "Well, the stars couldn't foretell their your own demise, could they?"

The shortage also pushed the paper's price so high that a resident wit remarked, "Why not sell it straight as raddi instead of going through the bother of printing the paper?"

THE GRINDING WHEELS OF BABUDOM

*Once it is inside its maw,
it proceeds like clockwork.
And it's as difficult to get off
as it was to get on.*

Large companies – and UN agencies – have notorious bureaucracies. They resemble the circles of Dante's *Inferno* or karmic cycles. With younger heads and computerization, things have changed somewhat, but a sanction is always incomplete without a hurdle. A new member of the perquisites club, an old employee with a changed status or anyone anywhere needing to get money from the establishment on a regular basis must go through the prolonged rigmarole of reminder and assurance before being inducted into the system. Once it is inside its maw, it proceeds like clockwork. And it's

THE GRINDING WHEELS OF BABUDOM

as difficult to get off as it was to get on. In the end 1970s Gautam Adhikari had taken a sabbatical from the TOI for a stint at Harvard. That was the Pull factor. The Push was that he had earned the ire of the imperious Giri. He was still being allowed to write, but on just about this side of redundancy.

However, when he went to the Editor with the news, Giri gave him a glowing letter of recommendation, offered him a paid column ('American Graffiti'), and even got the company to underwrite his air-fare to the US. In the preceding weeks, Giri had made a sort-of peace with Gautam because he needed to strengthen his own support base when Arun Shourie had been brought aboard by Samir Jain, firing on all cylinders – and in all directions.

Some time after Gautam took up the Harvard fellowship, the TOI's Washington correspondent JN Parimoo retired, and the post was offered to Gautam, who happily accepted. The terms were negotiated and agreed upon, but of course that was no guarantee that the money would start flowing. His reminders got more desperate since the Harvard stipend had been cut off, and he had a growing family to support in addition to needing funds to carry out his duties.

T Mannikan was Dr Tarneja's secretary, and like all PAs more powerful than the king when it came to nitty gritty. Gautam sent several telexes and finally phoned. Mannikan said soothingly, "Yesss, yess, your money will comuh." It didn't. Darryl, then the RE, was coopted, and he summoned the accounts people. With his nervous tic twitching in rage, he shouted, "YOU HAVE

TO SEND THE MONEY TODAY!" He banged the table so hard that the glass splintered, and blood oozed from his hand. The accountants turned pale. The money came.

There was also the issue of Gautam's books being shipped from Mumbai. Mannikan in his wisdom dispatched them to Seattle, Washington, instead of to Washington DC. The crate was ultimately rerouted to Baltimore and up the Panama Canal to the correct Washington. Who paid for this expensive tour? Babus in any clime are quicker to find ways to cover their own mess.

Babus in any clime are quicker to find ways to cover their own mess.

'When journalists were asked to beg, they chose to crawl.'

DARKEST HOUR, LIGHT MOMENT

On June 26, 1975, Indira Gandhi had declared Emergency, and with it came Press censorship, the only time in free India. It was the darkest hour, more so because as was later justifiably charged, 'When journalists were asked to beg, they chose to crawl.' The Censor held sway, and newspapers often appeared with blank swathes. But the iron grip was subverted on one memorable occasion.

A couple of days after the declaration, a notice appeared in the Deaths column: "O'Cracy, D.E.M, beloved son of L.I. Berty, passed away suddenly in Delhi on June 26. Deeply mourned by a large circle of grieving family and friends."

It was the idea of Ashok Mahadevan of the *Readers' Digest*, and he came in personally to the Classifieds section to place the insertion. The kindly desk clerk told him, "Sir, why such a long ad? It will cost too much, no. I can help you cut it to fit the minimum word length." Ashok balked, "No, no! I want it to appear exactly as it is. Cost is no object." He added with due solemnity, "He was a very dear relative of mine."

"I'm [Krishnamurthy] letting you go, but if you [Gautam Adhikari] have any problem, come back." That is absolutely the company's style. And no one really leaves the TOI, they just take a short break, and their heart and attention remains in the old home.

MOVING TIMES

In his first phase at BCCL, Gautam Adhikari had put in his papers shortly after he was made special correspondent of the fledgeling *Economic Times* in Kolkata. Krishnamurthy, who had taken over from Tarneja as GM at the Mumbai HQ, refused to accept his resignation, saying, "But we have just promoted you." Gautam told him "*The Hindu* is giving me Rs 1,000 more." His salary at ET at that time was Rs 1,500 so it was a huge jump.

Finally, Krishnamurthy relented, saying, "I'm letting you go, but if you have any problem, come back." That is absolutely the company's style. And no one really leaves the TOI, they just take a short break, and their heart and attention remains in the old home.

After three years, Gautam quit *The Hindu*, tempted by the mercurial MJ Akbar's offer of political correspondent and chief of bureau of *The Telegraph* which he was starting for the ABP. He joined, but realising he wouldn't be comfortable with Akbar's style, he resigned after the last trial dummy was printed.

MOVING TIMES

He called Krishnamurthy and asked, "Will you take me back?" "I'll get back to you," he was told. Soon enough Krishnamurthy called to say that Dr Tarneja (who had been elevated to MD) would be in Calcutta, and he should call him at the Park Hotel. Hannan Ezekiel, who had succeeded Rangnekar as ET editor, was with him. Hannan said, "We need an assistant editor at our main edition in Bombay who will shore up our political writing as well as banking and other sectors."

Gautam could even think of moving to that city of expensive real estate because senior editorial staff still got houses. He went home, seized his wife Rita by the waist, and spun her in a dizzy waltz.

He then remembered to check with his parents. "Will you be okay?" he asked. His father said, "What kind of nonsense question is that? The first chance you get to move out of Kolkata, you should take it. Start packing."

The allotted flat was at Hill Crest in Juhu. It may have been across the street from Amitabh Bachchan's bungalow, but the roof leaked. The company said they would fix it, and paint the rooms as well. They did. One yellow, one dark blue, and one a bilious green. Rita turned purple. "I can't live in this," she cried.

So Gautam went to the stern, gaunt and black-coated Mr T-for-Tight-fisted Pithavala and stammered, "The colours are not the problem, but the roof is pouring buckets. And, er, if you

*"The colours are not the problem,
but the roof is pouring buckets.
And, er, if you don't mind,
could you please re-paint the rooms?
All white will be fine."*

don't mind, could you please re-paint the rooms? All white will be fine." Pithavala surprisingly relented.

MOVING TIMES

However, in five months, in one of those rare cases where the landlord's position was upheld by the court, the Adhikaris' Bombay dreams were shattered. They were evicted. They found another dilapidated place. There were rats, it was musty, the plumbing kept breaking down – but it was on glamorous Pali Hill. Thus began in earnest a life greatly enriched by their Bandra friends, starting with Darryl D'Monte.

Government-shaking organisations must, and do, show a human side. When they were still in Juhu, Dr Tarneja, spoke to the principal of the Jamnabai Nursee school there for admission for Gautam's elder daughter, Priya, 5. Brinda, 2 ½, had been taken along to the interview because there was no one to leave her with, and she stood by sucking on a lollipop. The headmaster, said, 'Yes, yes, fill up the form. We like to have children of professionals. Ok, they are admitted."

"They?" Gautam began to ask, but Rita kicked him under the table. And, so with an ease that would make today's parents faint in envious shock, both kids had a school in Mumbai.

STATIONARY MOVEMENTS

The TOI has never stopped being a railway platform marked by the metronome of Arrivals and Departures.

Is the historic Victoria Terminus across the road to blame? The TOI has never stopped being a railway platform marked by the metronome of Arrivals and Departures. Dileep Padgaonkar's second of three departures was a mass movement. Matters soured between him and the Jains – some say there was too much of Dileep everywhere except where he was paid to be – and he left in 1994, taking a whole bunch of people, including Darryl, Badshah Sen and Arvind Kumar. Suddenly, for several months, the TOI ran on auto-pilot.

So now comes another return of the prodigal. Gautam Adhikari by then was a consultant with the World Bank and about to join it as a full-time staffer in a South Asia position. He got a call

STATIONARY MOVEMENTS

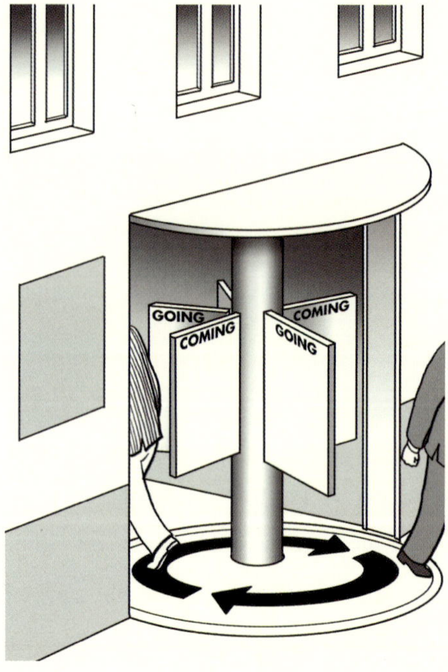

from Vijay Jindal, who had become part of the triumvirate with Pradeep Guha and Arun Arora, asking if he would be interested in returning to the fold.

Then he heard from the Chairman who said, "Come and have a chat with me. Not in Delhi, meet me in Bombay." So Gautam took the proffered ticket, and met Ashok Jain not in the Mumbai office, but in the extended family home of Shikhar Kunj on the city's aristocratic Carmichael Road. They talked over lunch and dinner, and breakfast the next day. There, the Chairman summarily said, "You can join us."

The departure is always the aberration. The arrival is always the homecoming.

They drove together to the office. Ashok Jain called a meeting of the department heads, and announced: "Gautam Adhikari is to be the next executive editor of the *Times of India*." Gautam would leave, return as edit page editor, leave. Dileep would return as executive managing editor, leave, return as consulting editor. The departure is always the aberration. The arrival is always the homecoming. Yes, the *Times of India* offers platforms of different kinds.

THAT BEAUTY CALLED DUTY

It gets more tempting when they have a paper with the reach of the TOI.

Managements everywhere often get carried away in somewhat ludicrous ways. It gets more tempting when they have a paper with the reach of the TOI. The Jains never ask to, indeed assiduously never want to, figure in the paper. They maintain a low public/social profile in any case, so none of their own photographs ever appeared till after the turn of the millennium when Vineet Jain began launching the new media products which demanded this kind of flash.

However, in 2001 after Nandita's numbingly premature end in a chopper crash near Itanagar, the family did agree to an obituary. Dileep Padgaonkar assigned Siddharth Varadarajan to write it, and since he was a comparative newcomer to the organisation, he was despatched to Arun Arora for details of the vivacious Nandita's packed brief life. He was then a director, also looking after Times Music, which was close to Nandita's heart.

When Siddharth parked himself opposite Mr Arora, notebook in hand, it triggered the Pavlovian managerial response. He started dictating. "Nandita-ji was joint managing director of Bennett Coleman & Co, Ltd. She was also the chief moving spirit of the sesquicentennial celebrations. The concert, Unusual Ragas, was one of its most memorable events. It was recorded and later produced by Times Music. It is available at Rs 85 per cassette, and Rs150 per CD…" A startled Siddharth looked up from his dutiful taking down, and asked "Sir, yeh bhi obit mein dalna hai, kya?" A slightly embarrassed Arora, quickly said, "Achha, rehne do. No need to include this."

*"VC is very upset.
What is this puff piece?
We don't publish such stuff."*

It is not only managers who overstep the boundary. The executive editor of the time was presiding over the morning meeting of the NMC (News Management Committee), and drew attention to a report on Soli Sorabjee, the noted constitutional expert, who had been given some legal award. He said, "VC is very upset. What is this puff piece? We don't publish such stuff."

The byline intriguingly was 'By A Special Correspondent' rather than 'By Our Legal Correspondent' which is how Rakesh Bhatnagar's unsigned pieces were credited. Siddharth, then handling the Bureau, said he would go through its list. Indeed Rakesh had filed, and when Siddharth asked him why he had done so when he was usually so correct about such matters, Rakesh replied sullenly, "What can I do, I was ordered to by…." And he named the executive editor!

THAT BEAUTY CALLED DUTY

But the call of duty can also cover with glory. We can talk of the peon Ram Lalji who cycled 30 km every day for 30 years to come to work. Or we can talk of bigger wheels. The structure of the editorial organisation in the post-Giri period was mostly free- wheeling and democratic. There were hierarchies and boundaries, but they were not difficult to negotiate. Siddharth pointed to the "flexibility which allowed a section head to push news coverage in a certain way. Our strong stand against the Gujarat government's shameful part in the post-Godhra communal riots of 2002 was the best example."

Kingshuk Nag, then Resident Editor of the Ahmedabad edition, was the commander in the field, and Siddharth, using his influence as head of the News Bureau, got those reports and news analyses full play in the paper. Jyotirmaya Sharma handling the Op Ed page provided strategic support. This concerted offensive gave the TOI a bold, critical profile it hadn't had in years. The BJP government is believed to have tried to get Shekhar Bhatia removed as executive editor. But the TOI could not be battened down. As Siddharth put it, "You can ignore a paper with a 30,000 circulation, but not one with two million. The Central government was forced to act."

"What can I [Rakesh Bhatnagar] do, I was ordered to by…." And he named the executive editor!

He added a footnote, “The VC, Samir Jain, kept completely out of all this, but referred to it in his elliptical way several months later. In the course of several rounds of the Sujagi garden while discussing a book on the Gujarat riots, he said, ‘I know we were critical in our coverage, and there was pressure from the PMO. But it didn’t bother me’.”

BUTTER TURNS TO JELLY

"It was unabashed and transparent bull, but you had to accept with grace the flattery he was pouring on to you."

Flattery is a legitimate corporate tool, deployed all over the world. On the editorial floor of Times House on Bahadurshah Zafar Marg, few were more skilled in this department than a sub who then rose to become Delhi's most visible journalism educator. He would come up face all aglow to the assistant editors and say, "Siddharth-ji, what a piece you have written! It reminds me of NJ Nanporia." Or, "Lolly-ji, what a piece you have written! It reminds me of Girilal Jain."

"It was unabashed and transparent bull, but you had to accept with grace the flattery he was pouring on to you."

JUNKETS? SUIT YOURSELF

They are always a source of heartburn and jealousy.

Junkets, the official invitations to visit different countries, are one of the great perks of what used to be a poorly paid profession. They are addressed to the editor as a matter of form, and he farms them out to the expert on that subject or occasionally to the journalist most deserving of a reward at that point in time. They are always a source of heartburn and jealousy.

In KK Dua's time, one such invitation came from Spain. Since it was a trade-orientation trip, it was offered to Sujit John, the assistant editor, who wrote on the economy. Sujit said, "Sir, I don't have a passport." Dua replied "That is a problem." Another member of the team jumped up and said, "I have a passport, and I've never been to Spain. Nominate me." Dua agreed.

"So, how was the holiday?" they asked him on his return. He spat out,"It was the worst trip of my life. Forget bull fights, one whole day was spent visiting a meat-packing factory. Forget senoritas in mantillas and fiery flamencos, another day was spent tramping through terminals and tarmacs organised by a company bidding for airports in India!"

JUNKETS? SUIT YOURSELF

The Grand Vazir of junketing is to be part of the media entourage when the Prime Minister/ President goes on an official visit abroad. This is the ultimate 'power trip' for journalists, or at least the political breed native to Delhi. But they can come a cropper.

Here's what happened when Mahendra Ved was nominated to go along with the President to some minor country. The standard MEA note attached to the invitation said, 'Please carry formal wear, bandgala preferred.' So Ved went to his boss, Monu Nalapat, saying that he didn't have one, and since the company was sending him, they should buy it for him. The Chief of Bureau sent him to Dileep Padgaonkar, who was then on his second innings, this time as Executive Managing Editor. 'Paddy', who should have known better, expansively said, "Excellent idea. Send me a note."

So Ved writes out one saying the company should pay for his bandgala, and Paddy moves it to VC – with predictable results. The request came back with Samir Jain's notation "Not only is there no question of a bandgala being charged to company account, why, in the first place is the TOI sending a journalist on such a trip." That effectively put paid to junkets of this genre for a long time.

The group is studiedly, even fiercely, non-statist. The President is a figurehead. His trips do not impact the reader, whose interests alone should decide the shots. In fact, the VC famously advised that the headline on the death of an elderly, ailing President should have a second deck saying whether and when a holiday has been declared.

He also circulated a copy each of a TOI of 1977 and one of 1997. It was clear that the earlier paper's 'customer' was the government and its ancillaries. It was full of official news and 'dais shots' that pandered only to sarkari egos. When Samir Jain entered the business, he had doggedly gone after editors to jettison this conventional approach, told them to get out of the ivory tower and cater to the reader instead. There had been resistance and scorn, but it was soon apparent that he had been the visionary. Every paper has followed suit.

Since this story began with a suit which the company refused to pay for, let's hear Siddharth Varadarajan's ploy to make the company pay for the trips he made. "It was always wiser to ask for the rupee equivalent since all forex payouts have to be sanctioned by the MD. I cottoned on to this when I wanted to go to Iraq in 1998. Subsequently, I covered the Yugoslav war in 1999, and an Afghanistan coming under the control of the Taliban. Everyone was surprised how I got so much money out of the company. This was the trick."

The Grand Vazir of junketing is to be part of the media entourage when the Prime Minister/ President goes on an official visit abroad. This is the ultimate 'power trip' for journalists.

Sid divulged his secret password to the treasury because he no longer needs it. He left the TOI in 2008 to take over the political bureau of *The Hindu* in Delhi.

THE TABLOID LIFE

Evening News provided the desperately sought 'time-pass', or even the shrill vicarious thrill in drab and monotonous lives.

Sharing space and reporters with the staid *Times of India* in Mumbai was the *Evening News of India*, which shut down on May 15, 1987. It was started to utilize the idle hours of the monster rotary machines on street level, and to mop up the advertising of the Mom & Pop retail trade and the cavernous cinema halls and weekend theatre. But it became a true-blue, 'red-top' with enough colour in its stories to compensate for the monochrome of the days of black and white newspapers.

It was the wild sibling of the staid *Times of India*, filled with the ill-gotten, the ill-tempered and the illicit, all the stock-in-trade of the tabloid universe. The city provided the two classical essentials needed to keep this raffish genre in business: a flourishing underworld and lesser crime plus the local trains on which hordes of commuters travelled to distant suburbs. *Evening News* provided the desperately sought 'time-pass', or even the shrill vicarious thrill in drab and monotonous lives.

Its team members not infrequently resembled the characters who usually featured in its headlines.

True, none of them was the 'Pydhonie Paanwalla' who routinely stabbed, axed or otherwise disposed of his wife's 'Panic-Stricken Paramour'. True, they may not have been involved in 'Fight Over Common Water Tap in Sewri Slum'. True, they would have been neither perpetrator nor victim in that tamer staple,'Ice Cream Vendor Relieved of Rs 16'.

But the *Evening News* reporters and desk hands certainly were habitues of the Aunty's joints which slaked Prohibition, and they frequented the dens of Bombay's notorious underworld to chat up their contacts and get their stories. They also had to fight constantly against falling into the trap of writing in the style of police station FIRs and in the jargon of their municipal and government beats.

"What you [reporters] got for me [K Kittu] today?" He wasn't asking for a quart of rum. Merely for the stories of house collapse, vendetta killings or slum fires, succinctly summed up as,'Gir gaya, mar gaya, jal gaya.'

The editor of *Evening News* was K Kittu. A short, bald man, he would collar reporters as soon as they came in with, "What you got for me today?" He wasn't asking for a quart of rum. Merely for the stories of house collapse, vendetta killings or slum fires, succinctly summed up as, 'Gir gaya, mar gaya, jal gaya.'

The news editor, US Rao, stopped short of improving Kittu's way of describing the turgid city's state of affairs, but he pounced with thundering glee on subs who used Indianisms with the frequency of raids on bars, brothels and businessmen. "Look at your headline," he would holler at some hapless youth who had written, 'Central railway trains pelted with stones by irate commuters.'

"I will pelt YOU with stones, you unschooled fool," he would rage, throwing the short slips of paper from the teleprinters back at him.

THE TABLOID LIFE

A chief reporter was quite a lad, going off on midday assignations with lady friends. But the problem was that he would soon find a new object of desire, and the old flame would burn the wires calling up for him. In the days before mobiles, they would have to do so on the office lines. Whenever someone shouted out, 'Phone for you," he would inquire if it was a woman at the other end.

Not verbally, lest his voice be heard and the person who had taken the angry call could not pretend that the chief wasn't in. The Casanova had a standard gesture for his gender query. He would jab his nostril with his forefinger, indicating the nose-stud that most Indian women still wore.

The racing column was one of the tabloid's most read. It was written by Pegasus, who in real life was Cecil Hendricks, a dapper Anglo-Indian with a penchant for white sharkskin jackets.

Busybee

But the *Evening News* itself was best known for its column 'Round and About' by Busybee which every single day, in 430 words, exposed the follies and foibles of a Mumbai still Bombay. It chronicled the city's low and high life like nothing before or since. It was compared to Art Buchwald's column in the *New York Times*, but it really was its own legend.

Behram Contractor, the man behind the pseudonym, looked the part, vague, stooped, thin to the point of being brittle, smoking as recklessly as he drank, viewing the world through soda-bottle spectacle lens, and wandering into the city's insalubrious gut to eat in the all-night joints after the graveyard shift. He made slumming fashionable as Mumbai's well-heeled were drawn, like moths to the charcoal grill's flame, by his descriptions of gritty kebabs and stews that had simmered for 24 hours in seven handis in squalid alleys.

Like Laxman's Common Man, he too had the Wife, her daily harangues his own surrogate comment. In real life, he was a confirmed bachelor always seemingly on the brink of dissolution. Then to everyone's surprise and the heartbreak of his many, mainly Roman Catholic girlfriends, he married the dynamic Farzana who changed his life – and his bohemian approach to it.

It [Round and About] was compared to Art Buchwald's in the New York Times, *but it really was its own legend.*

In his column, The Wife was ably supported by two sons, Derek and Darryl, with Bolshoi the talking Boxer being the philosopher of the family. The other regular was The Friend From the 21st Floor, Busybee's literary device for the city's burgeoning new-rich class. The now ubiquitous celebrities had not yet been spawned by a *Bombay Times* still to be born or they would have been dead meat in 'Round and About'. Instead, he took pot-shots at bloated politicians and arty crafty cineastes trudging to an obscure auditorium to watch a Cuban film, 'the hall filled with all two of them'. But he warmly toasted the Aunties who helped a generation of journalists, among others, through the ill-conceived era of Prohibition.

Behram in person could be more quietly cutting than his column and he had run-ins with several of his colleagues as well as those who were regular visitors to the *Times of India*. One of the latter was the eminent constitution lawyer AG (Ghafoor) Noorani (he of Laxman's 'patent leather hair'), a great friend and evening-walk companion of Khushwant Singh, then editor of the *Illustrated Weekly*.

The serious-almost-pompous Mr Noorani was not the kind of person you took liberties with. But Behram did so and in circumstances far less salubrious than a stroll down Churchgate. Those were the fractious days of the Emergency when any journalist worth the byline almost became extinct, and once fearless upholders of constitutional correctness lived in fear of the midnight knock.

THE TABLOID LIFE

One afternoon, Ghafoor was at the Weekly, a shadow of his usual stiff-backed bustle, when Behram shuffled up and said snidely, "What Noorani, you are not in jail yet?" The lid blew off the pressured Ghafoor, and he unleashed a steamed-up tirade. Behram of course remained unfazed, smirking and peering through his thick glasses, but the rest of the office froze in shock, wondering how best to restrain the lawyer should he punch that agent provocateur in the face. Fortunately, all he did was turn viciously on the heel of his perfectly polished shoes, and huff out.

"Why he got so angry?" asked Behram, blinking in artful innocence.

"Mr Godrej why are your new typewriters so bad? The keys keep falling off."

Soli Godrej, the eminent environmentalist and chairman of that respected family industrial empire, was also at the receiving end of Behram's disregard for occasion. Mr Godrej had just finished addressing a press conference on saving mangroves, or the tiger or the sarus crane or any of his many wildlife causes, when Behram unfurled his lanky frame and in his soft sibilant voice asked, "Mr Godrej why are your new typewriters so bad? The keys keep falling off."

Behram's chosen machine was a battered old Underwood, still tended as reverentially as a memorial by Farzana. In the office or even at home, he always sat on a stool crouched over the machine, hammering out his column in 30 minutes flat, well before the newsroom buzzed to life.

The *Evening News* went to bed at 11.30 am and was out on the street by 3 pm, well in time to spice up the tired and long commute back home on the 5.17 Fast to Borivali or any of the other packed locals of the Central or Western Railway. If Behram had been out bingeing till the early hours, he went straight to the office to type out his column, the walk there in the crisp dawn air clearing his brain.

Behram's chosen machine was a battered old Underwood, still tended as reverentially as a memorial by Farzana.

He exasperated this chronicler too, but only in proportion to her status as a recent entrant into the august domain of journalism itself, not just its grand edifice, the TOI. I was with the *Illustrated Weekly*, basking in the reflected glory of its unprecedented success under Khushwant Singh. I would tag along with Behram at lunch-time to try out some new hole-in-the-wall dive stirring up a biryani which rivaled the houris of Paradise. Flagging down a taxi on the way back, he'd tell the cabbie, "Times of India", and routinely turn to me and gloat, "If I say *Illustrated Weekly*, he won't know, no?"

But Behram Contractor was also the intrepid reporter of the *Times of India*, travelling to Bastar to cover the famine, to an Aurangabad erupting in Dalit riots, and to Khopoli, a pit-stop on the way to the hill-stations of the Western Ghats noted for its spicy, straight-from-the-frying-pan batata vadas till an adulterated hooch tragedy in 1971 gave it a less palatable notoriety. Behram reportedly did not take down any notes on any of these site visits, but on his return turned out unforgettable prose. He simply wrote what he had seen and heard, doing so from memory and from the heart. And he wrote it simply.

Vishwanath Sachdev, the amiable and highly successful editor of *Navbharat Times*. always told this Behram story to his own reporters. The Petroleum Minister of the time had called a press conference to announce measures for fuel saving during the oil crunch triggered by the latest West Asian crisis. It was standard stuff, and all the reporters filed more or less the same kind of story. Only Behram's had an additional sign-off line. It said, 'At the end of the conference, the petroleum minister drove off with his entourage in 20 cars.' "That," Vishwanath-ji said to his team, 'is the difference between a good reporter and a great one."

THE TABLOID LIFE

Behram Contractor left the Times of India in 1979 to start first *Mid-Day* with Khalid Ansari and then left that in 1985 to start his own, *The Afternoon Despatch & Courier*, taking his celebrated Busybee column with him. The buzz was that a petty news editor had refused to increase the extra payment for 'Round and About' from Rs 7 a day to Rs 10, even though the Evening News sold largely on this daily, deceptively simple column capturing the essence of Bombay.

Hard-driving, hard-talking, hard-working, Carol was, like her (unacknowledged) mentor, Behram Contractor, one of the true characters of the news room, with 24x7 professionalism and 24-carat heart.

THE NEWS FACTORY

The News Room was, and still is, a huge cavern as convivial as it is fraught when deadline approaches. In the Mumbai office of the '80s, it comprised the City reporters, and Sports and Business Desks of the TOI, the Evening News Desk, Maharashtra Times and Sunday Times with the clattering telex machines at each end and in the centre.

Someone or the other would be playing a prank, usually the deceptively mousy Srinivas Laxman, son of the legend, and known by his pet-name of Tikri.

The phone on the chief reporter's desk would ring, and picking it up Carol Andrade would furiously start taking notes of the 'big fire' that the caller said he wanted to report ('Citizen Journalism' did NOT arrive with breathless television). Then she would look up to find her juniors doubling over with laughter – they were the ones who had called her from another extension with a cooked-up story. Carol would, rant, rage and threaten to 'break your kneecaps'.

THE NEWS FACTORY

Hard-driving, hard-talking, hard-working, Carol was, like her (unacknowledged) mentor, Behram Contractor, one of the true characters of the news room, with 24x7 professionalism and 24-carat heart.

Journos always find some pretty juvenile ways to dissipate the nervous energy mounting up at edition-closing time. Should a keyboard fall or a hapless sub trip, the entire room bursts into applause.

Tension also sharpens hunger. The canteen boys still come around with the aluminum boxes of snacks slung across their shoulder as they have done for as long as anyone can remember. But the evening's idli, chevda, dhokla, nankhatai, samosa (and in Delhi kaley chaney or aloo tikki) need to be augmented.

In today's liberalised times, Mumbai office can order in a range of deliverables from fast-food menus pinned on their soft boards. The standard 6 pm halt, however, is at 'Bharati Café'. Bharati Dubey, the entertainment reporter, generously hauls in carrier bags full of packed farsan: thepla, kachori, cheeselings, khari biscuits, khakra which everyone flocks around, or dips into en route. This is augmented by home cooked sabzi-roti in tiffin boxes which is added to the community pool.

In Pradeep Guha's time as the director in charge of TOI, the entertainment beat became big and invitations to swanky cocktail parties would land on the chief reporter's desk. Anita Katyal recalled, "Three of us would troop in on one card. (Khalid Mohamed, later the feared film critic,) would say he was from TOI; Srinivas would say he was from *Evening News*, and I would pretend I was from *Femina*. No one would dare bounce us out for gate-crashing."

How could they when even press conferences are delayed till the all-important TOI reporter arrives?

"Three of us would troop in on one card. Khalid, not yet the feared film critic, would say he was from TOI; Srinivas would say he was from Evening News, *and I would pretend I was from* Femina.*"*

The dusky, lovely and committed Pamela Philipose worked for *Sunday Times*, and later married her left-leaning soul-mate, Achin Vanaik, a TOI assistant editor for many years before he forsook media for academia. Every time she pulled out a piece of paper, Behram Contractor would peer through his thick glasses and ask with his crooked smile, "You writing another memorandum?"

Inder Malhotra, the intellectually arrogant assistant editor who would become Delhi resident editor, incited the ire of Pam and her band of Protest Princesses for reducing a peon to a quivering mass of jelly in one of his usual fits of rage. This challenging of a top dog for the cause of the underdog did not go down well with her editor, Fatma Zakaria. Pam was given a 'punishment posting'; only the Comics page was allotted to her.

Girilal Jain spent 15 days of the month in the Mumbai office. While still trainees, Pam, Anita and a bunch of other girls requested an appointment with The Awesome Editor during one of these visits. His PA granted them an audience, and they timorously went into his room. They brightly gave their views on the state of the world and started saying, Sir, we would like to do this, that and the other. Throughout their enthusiastic torrent, Giri remained engrossed in the paper on his desk, periodically looking up peremptorily and filling his pipe. Recalled Pam, "We tried to keep up our very intelligent conversation, but gave up after 15 minutes, and sheepishly sidled out."

All sources share
an abiding desire for 'anonymity'.
They 'refuse to be named'.
They plead 'confidentiality'.

SOURCE FOR THE GOOSE

'Sources' are to a journalist what diamonds are to a girl, his 'best friend'. All sources share an abiding desire for 'anonymity'. They 'refuse to be named'. They plead 'confidentiality'. And they are willing to sing like canaries as long as they are guaranteed the protection of the cagey phrase, 'According to sources who spoke on condition of anonymity'.

However 'sources' is the most overused of words in a report, pulled out also when divulging the most publicly available information. It is a ploy to confer gravitas on a report cobbled together from a press release.

Sometimes, the source is extra extra special and in need of super protection. As the one tapped by a crime reporter in TOI, Delhi. He wrote in the report he filed, "According to sources close to sources...". It actually appeared in print this way, unexpurgated and unedited.

SOURCES

The Bureau's beats run more or less parallel to the Central ministries.

SENSE AND CENSUS

The Political News Bureau remains the aspiration of every journalist even though politics is no longer the sole Brahmin, and has had to contend with such erstwhile untouchables as local issues. Befitting its elevated status it has special correspondents, not mere reporters. Its beats run more or less parallel to the Central ministries. Naturally, it is based in the Delhi office. Bisheshwar ('Bish') Mishra usually covered the Union Home Ministry. So when the Bureau was doing a series on the census of 2001, he was dispatched to interview the Registrar General and Census Commissioner, Dr M Vijayanunni.

Bish began by asking him as basic a question as "How do you conduct a census?" The commissioner replied, "We count all the people during a given time." Bish demanded, "You mean you count every single person?" "Yes indeed," replied the grand official grandly. But Bish wasn't going to let him off that easily. He lobbed the next question in typical journalese, "What about elusive forest brigand, Veerappan? Will you count him too?"

Dr Vijayanunni testily replied, "Yes, if my enumerators find him, he will be counted." Our man had the last triumphant word, "When all the crack investigation teams headed by IGPs and police commissioners cannot find him, how will your people hope to do so?"

An earlier Bureau Chief was Monu Nalapat. He was a good boss, but he would say what he had to say, and then didn't want to prolong the conversation. He would absent-mindedly interject, 'Excellent, excellent!' You could be telling him that the President had just died, but it would have made no difference.

He [Monu Nalapat] would absent-mindedly interject, 'Excellent, excellent!' You could be telling him that the President had just died, but it would have made no difference.

One of his protégés was Prakash Nanda, a special correspondent covering the Ministry of External Affairs. Manoj 'Commander' Joshi, who took over from Nalapat, didn't think he was good enough for any slot in the Delhi bureau. He informed Paddy, who, in his special way, 'flattered to deceive'.

He told Nanda, "We want to move you to bigger things, so we are sending you as Guwahati correspondent." Trying to gild a remote and inconsequential posting, he laid it on thick, 'India now has a Look East policy, and Assam is the gateway to the whole South-east Asian region. From your vantage point, you will be writing on foreign affairs."

Prakash was first zapped, then he saw through the ruse and said he couldn't go because of medical reasons – he had a 'hole in the heart' which could cause serious problems at that altitude. He resigned gracefully.

Dina haughtily bristled, "Spies? What spies? There are certainly no spies in my department!" Arora looked distinctly alarmed. Had the CIA or the ISI itself infiltrated the TOI?

SPY-DER MAN

In the mid '90s, director Arun Arora, the earthy Personnel Manager DL Dhawan, the sophisticated Resident Editor Dina Vakil and Brand Manager Fawzia Madni held a grandiosely designated Recruiting Committee Meeting for TOI at 12 noon every Saturday. At one such RCM, Dhawan announced, "We have to do something about the problem of spies."

Dina haughtily bristled, "Spies? What spies? There are certainly no spies in my department!"

Arora looked distinctly alarmed. Had the CIA or the ISI itself infiltrated the TOI?

Fawzia, more familiar with Dhawan's accent, realized that he was referring only to 'sepoys', as peons are called in Mumbai.

No counter-espionage measures were called for. The threat was defused.

SCOOPING RUSHDIE...

"I'm here to play the boyfriend,"...

In December 2003, Salman Rushdie returned to his boyhood city, Mumbai, after a gap of 16 years. In between, he had written *The Satanic Verses* and been fatwaed into exile. So when he arrived at the Taj Mahal Hotel with the beauteous Padma Lakshmi draped on his arm, it was like a top secret mission. TOI was tipped off – no thanks to the literary grapevine – but via the Bollywood one: Padma was here to shoot a film. The TOI would be granted an interview as long as she was the focus. "I'm here to play the boyfriend," Rushdie besottedly murmured.

The interview team comprised three people: Resident Editor Dina Vakil, who had published an excerpt from *Midnight's Children* in the *Indian Express* and had met Salman when he was a young tyke, and was allegedly featured as Mina Vakil in *The Ground Beneath Her Feet*. The other was Rushdie fan Nina Martyris. Bringing up the rear was the veteran photographer (son of another veteran photographer) Shriram Vernekar.

Terrified that Shriram would innocently discuss the `scoop' with his photographer friends in other publications, Dina threatened him with dire consequences as her car drew up to the Taj. "I will kill you," was her (usual) refrain as she wagged a perfectly manicured finger in his mystified face. Shriram, whose stomping ground was the Sena shakha and Ganesh visarjan, didn't know what the fuss was all about.

SCOOPING RUSHDIE...

While shooting them, the genial Shriram did his best to put a slightly awkward Rushdie at ease, by engaging him in small talk. He lowered his camera, looked up at the celebrated writer and said conversationally, "First time in Mumbai?" Even as Dina rolled her eyes and looked like she wanted to throttle Shriram, an unfazed Rushdie twinkled, "Not quite."

... And Madonna

The CEO of the Times Group once called a correspondent to his office and told her about a secret mission that he wanted her to go on. It was the biggest scoop – not Netaji Subhash Chandra Bose or Elvis being sighted, but Madonna. She was reportedly lurking around Varanasi. The correspondent was told that she could not tell any one, not even in the newsroom. She went, and roamed around the streets of Varanasi for two days randomly (almost insanely) asking people whether they had seen the Material Girl. Instead, she found an enterprising sadhu who had perpetuated the myth.

JUGULAR ARTERY

If the edit page is the brain of the newspaper, then Jug made an effective neurosurgeon, cerebral, incisive, and with interests as manifold as the sulci on the cortex.

Jug Suraiya, known to the world as the hilarious columnist of Jugular Vein (and husband of the long-suffering Bunny) had a more serious day job as the editor of the edit page. He was the fourth incumbent after it was carved into a separate state of being, independent from the executive editor. His predecessors were the political analysts Dilip Mukerjee and Amulya Ganguli and the economics expert, Sanjaya Baru.

If the edit page is the brain of the newspaper, then Jug made an effective neurosurgeon, cerebral, incisive, and with interests as manifold as the sulci on the cortex. He spoke in grunts when he didn't want to be sociable, which was most of the time. But in the morning edit page meetings, he would be in full flow, or rather slow meander, holding forth in his 'quiet' way as he sat hunched in his chair, his long, bony fingers taking apart an idea, strand by strand.

His span ranged from Jungian archetypes to Michael Crichton's *The Andromeda Strain* to more quotidian chaos. His subject and mood would depend on whether he had electricity the previous night in Gurgaon, where he lived in the gingerbread-house media colony, and on the state of traffic on the long drive from there that morning.

JUGULAR ARTERY

Since his team of senior editors was equally eclectic, ranging from the science writer Mukul Sharma to the defence analyst K Subrahmanyam, the possibilities of discussion, and edit subjects, was infinite. Once in 1999, Siddharth Varadarajan arrived at the meeting in a state of great agitation, spluttering, "That gorgeous woman. How can she go off and marry this nonentity? She owes something to her position, to her fans, even to the country."

At first no one had a clue as to what he was getting so apoplectic over, and then they realized it was Madhuri Dixit, the reigning queen of Bollywood and muse to no less than the old master, MF Husain. She had announced her engagement to an obscure NRI doctor called Nene. The whole team was in splits at the absurdity of a man who normally wrote on such matters as nuclear proliferation and foreign policy getting so worked up over a film star. Siddharth, however, was dead serious, and refused to trivialise the development. So, Jug said, "Ok, if you feel so passionately about it, write an edit on it." Siddharth said, "Good, I'll do a third edit?" "No," clarified Jug, "I meant the lead edit."

*"That gorgeous woman.
How can she go off
and marry this nonentity?
She owes something
to her position,
to her fans,
even to the country."*

Sid did. He called it 'Runaway Bride', after the Julia Roberts hit film of the same year. It triggered an unprecedented avalanche of letters. The readers were obviously as upset over the mundane choice of their Heroine No.1, and Jug, being Jug, had been willing to subvert the lofty tradition of the first edit, and devote it to a subject closer to the reader's heart than to his own head.

K Subrahmanyam, the strategic analyst who was later appointed security adviser to the Government of India, had been dubbed 'Bomb Mama' by another member of the edit team, because of his hawkish stand. Jug was a total pacifist, and would tell him that "the only thing which will survive your nuclear holocaust is a cockroach".

"If you feel strongly against something that is the paper's line, if you have any ideological differences, feel free to refuse to write an edit on it. And feel equally free to write a bylined edit page article voicing your own opinion."

But his own beliefs never came in the way of allowing his team members to write on matters they felt strongly about. Conversely, he told them, "If you feel strongly against something that is the paper's line, if you have any ideological differences, feel free to refuse to write an edit on it. And feel equally free to write a bylined edit page article voicing your own opinion."

Vidya Subramaniam was as much a feminist as a political writer. Surprisingly, during the Monica Lewinsky scandal, she vociferously defended Bill Clinton, arguing that he was a much better President than his predecessors because "at least he was human". Jug said, "Since you are so convinced about this, write a by-lined piece."

He'd demolish the creative mystique by saying, "It's no big deal. Anyone can write on anything, and you can write an edit in 30 minutes." He did.

But Jug of course expected total silence in the room outside his cabin when he sat all scrunched up, writing out his pieces with a ballpoint pen. Once the decibel level rose to unacceptable standards and he slouched out, breathing fire, pulling the door so hard that the handle came out in his hand, which infuriated him even further. He flung it to the floor in a dark rage. On another occasion he vented his anger on the two edit page PAs, Murali and Venkat. He growled at them, "What are you two doing hanging around together like two parakeets on a perch?"

JUGULAR ARTERY

Jug was always notoriously aloof, refusing to acknowledge the existence of most human sub-species. On one famous occasion, a courier was standing around waiting at the desk of his secretary Sudha at just the mistimed moment when Jug shuffled out of his cabin to hand her his handwritten edit. The fellow committed the heresy of thrusting his register at Jug, expecting the deity to do something as commonplace as sign for a letter. Jug looked through him, threw his own sheet on Sudha's desk, and went back into his lair.

A few minutes later, he came out again to give Sudha another sheet. She still hadn't returned, but the courier boy was still there, and he repeated his 'heresy'. As the office watched in trepidation, Jug opened his third eye and reduced the sinner to ashes by ordering him to get out of his sight, with the added warning that if he caught him here again, he would call the police. So now you know the reason for the uncertain fate of the letters you couriered to Mr Jug Suraiya.

The most-told tale involves what else but an actual jug. A new peon entered his cabin wanting to change the drinking water, and diffidently said, "Sir, jug." Jug said, 'Yes, Jug. What do you want?" The bemused guy replied, "Ji, er, jug." This charade went on with a rapidly infuriated editor. Till finally the bearer had the sense to point to the object and say, "Paa-ni" as though to a slow child.

Naturally, the reclusive Jug never went to the Directors' Lunch Room. He usually brought his own low-cal, high-fibre sandwich or occasionally condescended to call for a tray to be sent down. He certainly did not go when a minister was invited to the DLR, and (churlishly) refused to participate in the gracious office practice of a cake being ordered and cut on every DLR member's birthday. He conceded just once, and came scurrying back in five minutes.

Narayani Ganesan, who joined the edit page in 1996, recalled that when she went on her first junket ("only to Khajuraho"), the other young journalists asked her "Who do you report to?" On being told, their eyes widenened with envy. "Jug Suraiya? So lucky! He's so funny. You must be having such a humorous time." Many years later she repeated the episode to him, by which time she had found the courage to add, "Huh! Little did they know what a grouch you are."

Vidya and Lolly had warned her at the start: "He's never effusive at any time, but never show him what you have written on a Monday." He always wrote his Jugular Vein first thing in the week, even though the column was scheduled to appear only the following Sunday, and, later, every Friday.

The sub-editors on the Desk were even more petrified. Vinita Nangia Dawra was still on those lower rungs when she came across the phrase, 'Ravana's tum' in Jug's copy while on the last shift. She didn't understand it, wasn't sure if it was a typo, but didn't dare call him up to ask, and certainly not at that late hour. When she encountered him in the corridor the next day, she did. He said, "Tummy" and slouched on without a pause.

Vidya and Lolly had warned her [Narayani Ganesan] at the start: "He's never effusive at any time, but never show him what you have written on a Monday."

Narayani Ganesan went on to handle the vastly popular Speaking Tree column on the edit page and then the entire Sunday supplement of that name. She too was all praise for Jug's consensual style, despite the long arguments which almost came to blows, and indeed led to walk-outs and much banging of doors.

Also despite the fact that she would get the shorter end of his notoriously short fuse because she would often be bored "when they were heatedly discussing the political stuff that went over my head". Catching her in mid-yawn, Jug would say tersely, "Narayani, if you want to sleep, please leave the room, and take a nap in your own cabin." Sometimes she did just that, following the first part of the directive if not the second. Anyone leafing through the newspapers at the meeting got the same marching orders.

JUGULAR ARTERY

And speaking of the 'Tree', you'd think such a philosophical- spiritual corner of the edit page would have attained moksha from controversy. It hadn't. One of the most contentious pieces turned out to be one by Bal Mukund Sinha, editor of the edit page of *Navbharat Times*, on a tradition in Bihar in which women were ritually beaten. The right-wing Vishwa Hindu Parishad sent a legal notice to TOI for publishing such a 'blasphemous piece that brought Hinduism into disrepute'.

Suits are all part of a day's work, since too many readers consider it their ordained right to get shirty over everything and take the paper's pants off.

On another occasion a contribution to Speaking Tree turned out to be a straight lift. Sudha Murthy, the redoubtable wife of Narayana Murthy, had written the original for a magazine and it was then to be included in the Chicken Soup series of books. The publishers threatened TOI with a legal suit. BCCL's lawyers, in turn, sent a notice to the plagiariser at the address he had given. It was in a remoter part of the Northeast. Too remote, in fact. The letter came back stamped, 'Returned to Sender. Addressee not found'.

Suits are all part of a day's work, since too many readers consider it their ordained right to get shirty over everything and take the paper's pants off. In fact there are individuals who scour every publication for this sole purpose. It is their full-time occupation.

'TOI has a Jojo and now the edit page has a yo-yo.'

In Jug's time, the edit page meeting room would be filled with the aroma of gourmet coffees, prepared in a proper French press. "Now it's only the wishy-washy dishwater from Mani's canteen," said Tam-Brahm Narayani, turning up her pert nose.

Gautam Adhikari, who returned to the TOI yet again, succeeded Jug. And Jug uncharacteristically sent out a message, 'TOI has a Jojo and now the edit page has a yo-yo.' According to Ganesan, "Gautam was more particular about form and protocol. He would meticulously post mortem the edit page. Jug could never be bothered to go into such nitty-gritty, but the heavens would certainly fall if there had been a shaming mistake."

And all Jug's editorial team-mates were glad that he stopped one hoary editorial page practice. "No one needs to hang around in the office. If you've finished your work for the day, you should leave." He certainly never stuck around to schmooze. Or else how would he read as prodigiously, watch the films he loved, and share a glass of wine with Bunny while feeding cheese straws to Brindle, the now departed mongrel bitch who alone of god's creatures Jug deferred to – slavishly?

BOMBAY BAWIS, DELHI DIVAS

Since the women [Bachi Karkaria and Dina Vakil] were both Parsis, the 'The Battle of the Bawis' had heavier artillery – and a degree of truth.

Pradeep Guha was more pasha than viceroy, but he was a great believer in divide and rule. Especially when it came to the senior women editors. He would tell Vinita Dawra Nangia, "Why is it that the women are always fighting with women? In Bombay, it's Bachi Karkaria and Dina Vakil. When I come to Delhi, it's you and Sabina Sehgal Saikia." Vinita recalled retorting, "Maybe it's the men who are cooking up these stories." He laughed – but continued to perpetuate the myth.

Goebbels-like it did become something of a self-fulfilling prophecy, playing on the insecurities which grip women as they confront the glass ceiling, making them view one another with suspicion and often open hostility. Since the contenders would be no more than two, it became more intense. In Mumbai, the positions occupied – and eyed – were more senior, and since the women were both Parsis, the 'The Battle of the Bawis' had heavier artillery – and a degree of truth.

It may have been just circumstance but it looked pretty much like design to the paranoid protagonists when management decisions seemed tailored to sharpen these rivalries. At one point,

Guha covertly hinted that though the 'Bombay Bawis' had significantly helped the TOI evolve to its present shape, neither could be made executive editor because the other would be implacable – and, shrug! – she was equally indispensible.

Sure, there would have been the mother of all tantrums, but the 'cats' would have been smart enough not to let some other 'monkey' run away with the chappati while they squabbled. The 'loser' would have ultimately been gracious enough to have conceded, if not for the sake of the sisterhood, at least with the face-saver of an acceptable compensatory responsibility. This would have been perfectly possible in such a many-faceted organisation.

But it was all shadow boxing, the matter was never officially broached, so the women had no opportunity to present their views or sort it out between themselves. Besides, for the grinning bystanders, reconciliation would be more boring than recrimination; if the biwi-biwi were razi, then what fun would there be for the qazi?

If the biwi-biwi were razi, then what fun would there be for the qazi?

Matters spun out more overtly in the case of the Delhi Divas.When Delhi Times was started, Sabina Sehgal Saikia was made its editor, but Vinita was given charge of its *raison d'etre* – Page 3, and the fashion and relationships sections. Vinita had no reason to rejoice either because, having done a good job as Saturday Times editor, she felt she should have been given full charge of the new babe on the block.

Worse, the best columns from ST were moved to DT on the argument that the new paper needed to be propped up. And who would sign off the dual-responsibility pages? The line of command was left vague because no one wanted to incur the wrath of either of these feisty prima donnas. It predictably led to constant friction. They were legitimate, gender-neutral, work-place problems, but they were always dismissed as the 'the usual petticoat war', and left unresolved which aggravated the enmity.

SATURDAY TIMES FEVER

*When it was launched,
it featured anything and everything,
including a story on Chandni Chowk
as a hub for selling and hiring
out public address systems
and their accessories.*

When Pradeep Guha took over Saturday Times, he would summon the respective editors in charge to Mumbai for a review and course correction every few months. Amy Fernandes was based there so she simply carried on with what she was doing till the 'summons' finally came. But Vinita Nangia from Delhi and Ingrid Albuquerque from Bangalore would hang around all day on an empty chair if they could find one. Then, when they were weary, fed up and over-caffeinated on all the tea and coffee they had downed in boredom, "He would call – and give us all of five minutes at the end of the day."

At Saturday Times, Vintia had picked up enough of the rag trade to have been named 'Delhi's best fashion writer' but in the early days, it was more pins than cushions.

When it was launched, it featured anything and everything, including a story on Chandni Chowk as a hub for selling and hiring out public address systems and their accessories.

Then, Vineet Jain, who had returned from his Swiss college and had begun easing into the business, realized that it would go nowhere without a clear brand positioning. He decided on the three F's of Fashion, Food and Fun. Saturday Times was being handled by the willowy Prabha Chandran, who had worked at Femina in Mumbai when she was still Prabha Kripal Singh, had then moved to Delhi along with her husband Ramesh. But Dileep Padgaonkar was executive editor of the mother paper and he distributed portfolios in ST 'like a raja flinging coins'.

He [Vineet Jain] decided on the three F's of Fashion, Food and Fun.

"Vinita, you take Fashion," he said as expansively as a Lycra lord. "I don't know the first thing about it," she protested. He replied, "We don't want you to know, we just want you to get the designers to write." That sounded as easy as pulling up a zipper. But it got stuck.

The Rohits, as in Bal and Khosla, said, "Darling I would love to write, but I don't have the foggiest idea how."

Suneet Varma said, "Come over. I'll talk, you write."

Martand Singh 'Mapu' said, "Come be a fly on the wall of my studio. You'll learn a lot."

Ravi Bajaj said, "Always judge a designer by the inside of his seams."

Ritu Kumar gave a tip or two of her own.

Prabha, said, "Trust your own instincts. If you think something is good, praise it. If you think it stinks, sink it."

So, with a little help from her friends, Vinita got by. And well.

Soon, she was in charge of Saturday Times, and gave it a cheeky style. One day Dileep called her, and said, "Look, I want humor writing but not humour writing by you. Believe me it's very difficult." Vinita agreed, "Yes, see how grumpy it has made Jug!" Everyone burst out laughing and Padgaonkar smirked and said, "Very naughty!" But he was the one who had to face the music.

SATURDAY TIMES FEVER

One Saturday, a picture of a model wearing a white shirt unbuttoned to reveal a lacy black bra had appeared with the caption, 'Booby Trap'. Saturday was also the day that the TOI executive editor and his honchos went out to meet the public in an outreach program designed to boost the paper's image and circulation. That morning it was the turn of a traditional, middle-class Delhi colony. The straitlaced readers jumped on him for ruining a family paper and threatened to cancel their subscriptions. He came back, called in Vinita and told her, "Excellent headline, but you will never, ever, ever give one like that again."

However, there was a time when in hindsight she agreed with Padgaonkar's disparaging of her sense of humour. That was when she had carried a piece on the duo behind the grisly 'tandoori murders' and titled it 'Hot Couples'. The editor, with pun intended or un, had branded it as being 'in very bad taste'.

In Delhi Saturday Times sat in a corner of the 3rd floor newsroom which was a loud, bustling office, bristling with egos. Badshah Sen would shout abrasively from one end of the room at the larger-than-life Sabina Sehgal Saikia, who would give it right back to him, and louder, across the hall.

Sabina, would became an internationally acknowledged food critic. She certainly knew her onions – and asparagus – at the start more than Vinita did about fashion, but she stumbled into the role as accidentally as her rival in the 'Duel of the Delhi Divas'.

Jiggs Kalra used to write the food column for the *Times of India*, having started it in *Evening*

News. But his recipes always had a mile-long list of ingredients which you would have to travel even longer to procure. One day, Vineet Jain felt there should be a restaurant review column in Saturday Times. Raminder Singh, then resident editor of TOID, was summoned and told to get it going.

"Where will I find a restaurant reviewer?" he despaired. VJ said, "Think of someone who loves cooking and loves eating." When Raminder was returning to his room, still grumbling, he saw Sabina, then a crack correspondent in the political bureau. Voila! Here was his woman. She always brought tiffin carriers full of delicacies for everyone.Vinita would later add a sniffy correction: "Only for the guys."

Here was his woman. She [Sabina Sehgal Saikia] always brought tiffin carriers full of delicacies for everyone. Vinita would later add a sniffy correction: "Only for the guys."

He asked, "Will you?" Spunky Sabina replied, "Why not?" After the first column appeared, she was stunned. "I can't believe it," she said. "I've never got this kind of response for any of my major political stories, not even for my ground-breaking interview with the Dalai Lama." Thus, another star was born.

***

And speaking of food, when Indu Jain was scheduled to visit Hyderabad, Jyotirmaya Sharma, then resident editor there went ballistic over his 'lists'. He, Vinita Nangia, who was looking after Hyderabad Times, and Anil Kumar, the branch head, all scoured the city trying to source the exotic fruit that Jyotirmaya said, "Chairman must have." They asked the hotels. They shook their heads, "No, we don't keep kiwi and dragon fruit, but for you we can fly them in. Do you have four or five days?" They didn't, but somehow a respectable enough fruit basket was assembled. Chairman hadn't asked for any of this, so she was delighted all the more.

WHEN THE MD BROKE A STORY

and even put it on hold

Vineet Jain rolls up his sleeves – meticulously in v. neat folds – and buckles down to the nitty gritty in all the media that exercises him at that time. He even orchestrates news stories on *Times Now*, as he did during the rescue of Prince, the little Rajasthani boy who fell into an open 60-ft-deep borewell in 2006. His social connections enable him to add muscle or masala to a report. And on one memorable occasion, the MD actually broke one of the big news story of 2009: That Manu Sharma, the politically connected main accused in the high-profile Jessica Lal murder case, was out on parole ostensibly to meet his ailing mother, but actually partying.

HELLO....
HELLO....
TRRR
RRRRR
RRRRR

The arrogant fellow wasn't even keeping his head down. He drew attention to himself by getting into a verbal fight with the son of the Delhi police commissioner, YS Dadwal, at the F Bar of Ashoka Hotel and then, along with his apparel-exporter friend, Salil Dhingra, walked into the Lounge & Party (LAP), at the adjacent Samrat Hotel. The police arrived, Manu managed to slip away, but they picked up Dhingra and, as in a Hindi movie, mistakenly also hauled off business tycoon Samir Thapar. Who called Vineet Jain. Who summoned a reporter from Delhi Times and even went along with him to LAP. Since he's a regular there, he knew that he could make them as well as the F Bar management talk more openly.

WHEN THE MD BROKE A STORY

The MD was on the case like a proper newshound. He alerted Vikas Singh, the Delhi RE; he told the DT reporter not to file the story till he had vetted it himself. He then called Vikas again, and told him to hold the story because "there's too much hearsay. Tell the reporter to go back and get the bar manager's quotes. On tape, and clandestinely if necessary."

In the meanwhile, Vikas had a run-in with his immediate boss, Jojo (executive editor Jaideep Bose), who was hollering on the line from Mumbai pressuring him to release the story for all editions so that no one else out-scooped the TOI. Vikas told him, "The reporter says it will hold." Jojo thundered, "Who the hell is this reporter?" Vikas replied "MD". He also recalled that Vineet called him "five times that night with great quotes".

He has the informality
of a pet name.
What formality can you expect
from a man who is known
only by his daak naam, Jojo.

JOJO A-GO-A-GO

In one generation, editorial style has made a 180-degree turn. If you were to suggest to Jaideep Bose that he is the adviser to the prime minister he would give you one of his don't-talk-bull looks, guffaw and sidle off to the Desk, not to advise but to get cracking on the first lead headline. He has the informality of a pet name. What formality can you expect from a man who is known only by his *daak naam*, Jojo?

He will tell his RE in the morning, "The edition must go on time tonight." Then at 10 pm, he'll go sheepishly to him and say, "Don't shout at me, but I'm going to change the front page." He is arguably the most hands-on editor that TOI has ever known. And the most mobile. He moves from edition to edition depending on where a big story is breaking.

JOJO A-GO-A-GO

Every night, he will be out there, pacing impatiently from bureau to reporters to newsdesk, and then parking himself at the terminals, designing the page, cogitating over the most telling lead picture, and, with the senior team massed around him, evolving memorable headlines. He leaves with the night shift. Or later. He arrives with the morning shift. Or earlier.

'The Crest Edition', the latest from the TOI and a global journalistic landmark, is Jojo's baby.

He was made executive editor of the stiff-suited *Economic Times* when he was just 29. He loosened its tie. In 2004, he was moved from ET and given charge of TOI. In 2008, the post of Editorial Director was created for him, and Arindam Sen Gupta, the RE in Delhi and one of his closest colleagues right from his ET days, took his place as executive editor.

'The Crest Edition', the latest from the TOI and a global journalistic landmark, was Jojo's baby, playground and magnificent obsession. Even after its circulation was bounding northwards within weeks of its launch on September 26, 2009, he continued to position himself in Delhi while whipping up ideas and contributions from his teams across editions, making everyone do their utmost. They do it because Jojo leads from the front, and pats on the back (often with a long sms that can run into six parts).

It was the same while orchestrating his big offline ideas, notably Lead India (2007), Teach India (2008) and Aman ki Asha (2010), the bridge-building initiative in collaboration with Pakistan's leading Jang media group.

He has certainly made this the secondmost challenging job in the country, but now the emphasis is on the word, 'job', and not 'country'. That's his personal style as well as the policy of a paper which actively chooses to 'put society before state'.

The way he chose the lead picture for the cover story on Sachin in Crest when Tendulkar completed 20 years in test cricket is typical. The idea was to show Sachin growing from genius to legend. Scores of photographs were downloaded from Comyan, the picture archive. Several more opinions were taken. Jojo kept talking it out. Then ultimately he decided to go for the one of the starry-eyed boy which everyone else had rejected.

JOJO A-GO-A-GO

It was an emotional sixer of a photograph, and it outdid another historic great: Sachin, looking heavenwards with his arms spread out across all seven columns of the front page in a Christ-like pose. This was after he scored his first double century, in Australia in 2001. It was published in ET. Its executive editor then was, again Jojo.

THE ECONOMY-SIZED BUDGET EDITION

It deconstructs the Finance Bill into segments relevant to the reader in all his/her avatars.

Every major Jojo project is undertaken with the strategy, tactics, planning – and subterfuge – of The Great Game. But nothing surpasses the grand, 70 mm, multi-starrer, cast-of-thousands Budget edition. It is a massive exercise. It deconstructs the Finance Bill into segments relevant to the reader in all his/her avatars: as corporate leader, tax payer, and as a consumer of commodities, FMCGs, big-ticket items or quality of life. It proceeds to cram these pages with as much information, analysis, expert-speak and trend-tracking. Finally, all this is packaged readably and attractively.

THE ECONOMY -SIZED BUDGET EDITION

The undertaking begins with the editorial equivalent of the cosmic 'Aum': Jojo's ritual incantation, "This time it'll be a simple edition." His close aides roll their eyes upwards. Then he starts getting excited. With his think tank, he has conversations that can go on for six hours. "My wife delivered our daughter in less time," muttered an exhausted participant after one such cerebral marathon.

In a dissipation of nervous energy, it meanders from cricket to politics to nostalgia. Every 15 minutes or so someone brings the discussion back to the agenda. P Ram, Ajit Ninan, Neelabh Banerjee, each of the TOI's star artists, sends his list of concepts. They range from the classic to the utterly bizarre. But nothing is too conservative or too whacky to consider. Or even make it. Each edition has to surpass the previous one in appeal. Each year it is a tougher act.

"My wife delivered our daughter in less time," muttered an exhausted participant after one such cerebral marathon [for the Budget Edition].

Five or six versions of the front page are prepared. The Star Chamber reassembles. And Jojo says, "Ok, which?" Let's say you point to 'C'. He'll hem and haw, "Ya, but don't you think 'D' is more original?" You come round to his point, and agree. Then he'll say, "But the problem with it is …" Two hours later you get to 'A', which is what he had decided on from the start.

When someone protests in despair, "Jojo, why don't you simply pick what you like rather than make us go through all this?" he will look seriously offended and say, "What do you think this is? A dictatorship?" Indeed, there is huge teamwork, all shades of opinion are sought and taken, but, at the end of the day, it's one hyper-energetic man – and mind.

It's suspected that Jojo starts planning the edition even before the FM starts planning the Budget.

It's suspected that Jojo starts planning the edition even before the FM starts planning the Budget. It begins with the inner core, then over the weeks, the concentric circles start fanning out in widening circumferences. The templates are preloaded with panels, boxes, infographs, tabulations, statistics and trivia that make each Budget edition so complete. Some are ready to heat and eat on the actual day; others will need the addition of the key ingredient which can be acquired only from the FM's speech.

There are more dummies than at a ventriloquists' convention. Hundreds of potential photographs are downloaded, especially those that lend themselves to smart 'kickers', the catchy phrase which leads into the caption. Lists of alternative headlines for the different components of a budget, from autos to zippers, are made beforehand. Everything is neatly classified in the mounting stockpile.

If anyone is busier than the editorial director it is the PA whom he shares with the executive editor. The cherubic Sanjay Kalia keeps track of this inventory, and sends out the master document of instructions and all its zillion appendices to the infantry of reporters, the captains of their beats, the brigadiers on the Desk, and the GOC anchoring the operation at each edition centre.

Then, in the last week, star writers and crack desk hands from different editions start arriving to deal with the copy, write, tweak and rewrite brilliant headlines, and ensure that no false note however slight dares creep into this orchestrated masterpiece.

"What do you think this is?
A dictatorship?"
Indeed, there is huge teamwork,
all shades of opinion
are sought and taken,
but, at the end of the day,
it's one hyper-energetic man
– and mind.

One year the headline given was 'Thanda-garam.com' dismissing a tepid Budget. The finance minister himself riposted with a publicly aired defence, saying, "No it's garma-garam."

THE ECONOMY -SIZED BUDGET EDITION

One of the most memorable front pages featured not the usual elaborate Neelabh / Ninan visual, but a black and white photograph. Not any photograph, but a Cartier = Bresson one saying a thousand words as it captured the cone of the sophisticated PSLV being transported on a primitive bicycle to the satellite launch site at Sriharikota. As usual twenty headlines were thought of, and honed down to two. 'Flying Economy' and 'Cruise Control' since 'Lose Control' from Rang De Basanti was the big hit number at the time.

Jojo was underwhelmed by Choice No 2 because his eclectic range of interests doesn't include Bollywood. To everyone's impressed surprise, the very correct, restrained and Bengali metro editor, Subhendu Mukherjee, at 12 midnight broke into a rendering of 'Lose Control'. However he couldn't make the desired impact because the critical background score of all AR Rahman numbers was beyond the bandwidth of the denizens of the Delhi newsroom.

Jojo, in his cynical drawl, said, "I don't quite see what the big fuss is all about." However, as Vikas recalled, "After all that, we could as well have left the headline space blank because no one paid much attention to it. It was only remembered as the 'Bresson edition'."

Every year, at least three alternative Front Page themes and their visuals are ready and tremulously waiting to take centre stage. They are still veiled from all but the most need-to-see eyes. Then, like a bride sailing up the aisle on her father's proud and nervous arm, the chosen one will be sent to the main make-up terminal in the newsroom to collective (and mandatory) gasps of awe. The others will not be unceremoniously jilted. Each one is a creative beauty, and will be used elsewhere in the Budget edition.

THE ECONOMY -SIZED BUDGET EDITION

And after scores of suggested headlines and variations, after the frenetic high of the last hour, you may go home bleary-eyed and assuming it's all been tied up – only to find something quite different when you stagger to your door the next morning to pick up THE EDITION. Jojo has managed to come up with yet another improvement almost as the file 'stepped' on to the giant machines.

Despite being such a veteran of the Budget edition, Jojo is still very nervous during the twilight zone between the pages being fired to the press and the paper hitting the stands, or doormats. He gets into his version of depression, which is deeply reflective. His team makes the appropriate noises as if calming a colic baby, "It's brilliant. Don't worry, by 9 am your phone inbox will be flooded." The Brand director, Rahul Kansal, is usually the first to sms, and it's usually something as understated as 'Awesome. How do you surpass yourself each time?'

In 2009, the clock had digited past 10.00, and there wasn't a single congratulatory sms from Kansal in Vikas Singh's inbox. The suspense was killing so the Delhi RE came to office in trepidation and haste. He found Jojo with a beatific smile. "So is your inbox full?" Vikas asked. "Thrice over!" was the reply with the usual repressed beam. Vikas cornered Kansal in the lunch room, and demanded, "Why didn't you message?" "Oh, it was so terrific that I presumed everyone would have congratulated you, and I thought why add to the jam?" He was soundly berated. "You established the form; please don't deviate from it."

There are two immutable, non-negotiable, non-breachable constants in the Budget edition. The first is the 'Wow' imperative. The other is secrecy. The second is the more overwhelming, and borders on the farcical.

Those working on the main visual are put inside rooms with locks, the glass panes are papered over, and to enter you have to knock thrice and give the verbal code. It could be something as silly as 'Lal Gulab'. Seriously. But despite all this, security has been breached, people have unwittingly barged in, and wondered why their innocuous act has been met with faces paling and papers being hurriedly shoved into drawers.

Take what happened in 2009. The 'pink chaddi' campaign was launched by a group of Bangalore women as a counter to the Shri Ram Sene's warning against celebrating Valentine's day, and snowballed into a mass liberation movement. Since V-day came just a fortnight before B-day, it was decided to use these as icons for the 'Consumer' page of the Budget edition. But when you search for pink panties, the Net ejaculates a whole lot else on to your screen. So when an intruder enters your room, you try desperately to shut down the computer, which makes it all look even more hanky panky. Or hanty-panty. That's exactly what happened.

If you hear a 'Shhh' in the loo, it's not on account of someone persuading a baby to pee, it's Jojo cautioning a careless colleague who has starting talking about that RAW document known as the imminent Budget edition while lined up at the pissoirs. Someone in one of the closed cubicles 'might overhear'.

"Oh, it was so terrific that I [Rahul Kansal] presumed everyone would have congratulated you [Vikas Singh], and I thought why add to the jam?"

On another occasion, having gone through this whole secrecy rigmarole of locking up people and layouts, by some fluke the dummies landed up in the general network for all to access. Jojo went ballistic. How to start from scratch again at this late stage? Someone had the bright idea – and did convince him – that "no one will believe that we've left all this out in the open by mistake. They'll think it's a decoy, and ignore it."

THE ECONOMY -SIZED BUDGET EDITION

On an even more red-faced occasion, after the penultimate Budget meeting between Systems, TOI and ET, one of the Systems guy casually handed a CD to Jojo, and said, "This was left behind on my desk when you came for a test run last night. He added "We all had a look and think the edition will look stunning." Forget cloak, Jojo was all dagger and disbelief that his efforts at secrecy could end in such carelessness. What was that about 'the best laid plans of mice and men'?

Who is after the top secrets of the TOI Budget edition? From whom are all these pages being protected? International spies? Finance Ministry flunkies? Rival media houses? Nah! In an unintended version of the boast that the Times competes only with itself, the enemy lies within. Jojo's main anxiety is his former fiefdom, ET. And the ET executive editor returns the compliment.

In outdoing each other, the two papers have begun to think like each other. After all, the jazzy Budget edition genre was created by Jojo when he presided over ET. So, one memorable year, by some strange, subliminal coincidence, both papers used the visual of the multi-bladed Swiss knife. The TOI's provisional headline had been 'Mr Fix-It Screws It'. So, who got fixed? Who found the screwdriver? The Geneva Convention ordains that our lips are snapped shut.

The edit page team sat in a rarefied enclave carved out of the bustling newsroom on the 3rd floor of Times House in Delhi. It had the most of these monikers.

GAME OF THE NAME

Over the years, many people were referred to by other names. Some of them were necessarily encoded, such as 'Borealis' for Arora, bestowed by RK Laxman. But some were benign, intra-departmental, used openly, and delighted in as much by the object of their attention.

The edit page team sat in a rarefied enclave carved out of the bustling newsroom on the 3rd floor of Times House in Delhi. It had the most of these monikers. Among these were 'Commander' for Manoj Joshi because he was the expert on security&military matters; he also had an authoritarian, don't-mess-with-me manner. And 'Bomb Mama' for K Subrahmanyam, the senior editor who was an acclaimed authority on defence.

Bomb Mama was a diabetic, and had to eat at short intervals. So he would noisily unwrap candy while firing esoteric details of weaponry. He was also later diagnosed with cancer, but he extracted humour from his agony. He devised a code word for the long painful sessions with topmost management: 'Chemotherapy'.

GAME OF THE NAME

Vinod Taksal was called 'Taxalite' because he was, as Siddharth ('Sid') Varadarajan, described him, a 'salt of the earth' kind. Shastri Ramachandran was 'Monster', soon abbreviated to 'Mons', because he was constantly harassing his colleagues to produce 200-word items for Current Topics. He was in charge of this rather dull section at the bottom of the edit page.

'Paddy', Dileep Padgaonkar, came up with 'Holy Messenger' for Jyotirmaya Sharma. This was not only because this wickedly jovial senior editor wrote on matters Vedic and philosophical, but also because he was the conduit between their own 3rd floor and the 4th floor, the sanctum sanctorum in which were installed the Jains and directors. The Holy Messenger would be the bearer of glad or not-so-glad tidings from above.

Paddy also coined the Watergatesque 'Peep Throat'. This was his inspired name for Prathyush Kant, the metro editor in Delhi on account of his tall claims of access to high functionaries – inside and outside the office. In a capital city comprising almost solely of fixers and 'fixees', the promised contacts couldn't be any old 'con'.

Obviously, 'The Luminous One' for the highly evolved VC was restricted to the closed circle.

Jug Suraiya wasn't honoured with a nickname during the years that he headed the edit page simply because his own monosyllabic one caused so much confusion, and not only vis-a-vis the hapless water bearers of the editorial floor. A correspondent once referred to him as Jagat Murari.

In his native Kolkata, most people pronounced his name 'Joog', as in the Bengali way of saying 'Yug'. But he himself loves to tell the following story.

He had gone to the city's most phamous Bengali homoeopath (of course, in the inseparable company of Bunny) and had kept waiting for his turn in that cavernous hall hanging heavy with hypochondria. He fidgeted impatiently for two hours, and then collared the dhoti-clad receptionist, vociferously demanding to know why he was still being made to hang around when those who had arrived much later had already been granted entry into the inner chamber of the Daktar-babu.

Jug Suraiya wasn't honoured with a nickname during the years that he headed the edit page simply because his own monosyllabic one caused so much confusion.

The Bengali intermediary looked at Jug's token number, tallied it with the list in front of him, and launched his own offensive. "Aapni ki nonsense bolchhen! Bhawt do you mean I deed not call you? I announced your name three times, like thees..." And he repeated loudly, "Yug Shoorjo, Yug Shoorjo, Yug Shoorjo!"

***

Many years earlier, on the 4th floor of the Mumbai building, Khushwant Singh's fun-loving team was the hyper-active labelling machine. The Weekly could amuse itself with the passing pageant of people from other departments because it occupied a strategic position close to the toilets which were then tucked away at the deep end of the hall instead of their current isolation near the lift landing.

Qurratulain 'Annie' Hyder, the formidable intellectual with a skittish-schoolgirl sense of humour was the Weekly's unchallenged nicknamer. The Times has always had an awesome Reference Library, now tech-ed up as the Times Archives and Knowledge Centre. For many years, it also had a 'Research Department', headed by the Mahatma's suave grandson, Arun Gandhi. Annie promptly 'honoured' him with 'Grandson of the Nation'.

GAME OF THE NAME

Gandhi's 'harem' comprised a motley group of women with varying intellectual capabilities. One of them was a slim Sindhi who obviously had a hectic social life because she found it difficult to complete her morning's ablutions in time to 'catch the muster'. All staffers, other than those in the two topmost grades, were pitted against this register which could ruin their day with a red cross. So, some came gobbling their breakfast in the lift or put on their eye make-up at their desk. But this young woman alone actually brushed her teeth in office.

Ms C would sashay up from her 3rd floor office to use the larger mirror in the 4th floor women's toilet. She fancied kurtas with faux leather-trim, so Annie with a sidelong glance of her kohl-lined eyes would say in a stage whisper, "Here comes Revolver Rani". The name came from a then current Hindi film.

Dharam Vir Bharti of *Dharmyug* became 'Al Capone' because of the cigar dangling from his mouth. The unexpected giver of this name was the quietest member of that rambunctious assembly, Elizabeth Rao.

The Weekly's own had their own. 'Ma Zacks' was Fatma Zakaria to the irrepressible youngest duo of 'Jiggs (Jai Inder Singh) Kalra and 'Biks (Bikram) Vora. Ramesh Chandran was 'Bang Bang', but no relation to 'Revolver Rani'. He got this name from the four-year-old son of a colleague whom he always greeted with a cowboy routine every time they met at the Mandwa clubhouse of the Bombay Sailing Association. The name dropped anchor at the office.

One day, a sub called out to Raju Bharatan, the crossword-maker and font of every cricket statistic known to man, saying "Ra-ju Bha-ra-tan, phone for you!" Bharatan looked up, fingering his nose from side to side as was his wont, and said archly, "I detect a note of irony in your voice." So he promptly became 'The Irony-Detector'.

'Bhagwad Gita' also originated in a phone call. The Tamilian Geetha was trying to convey her name to the guy at the other end of the line. She even spelt it out, but he was clearly unfamiliar with the extra 'h' used by South Indians. In desperation, she shouted, "Gee-tha, as in Bhagwad Gee-tha." After this episode, we always referred to her thus – but always behind her self-important back.

On a less sanctified plane, Ben Costa became 'Kabb-babs'. This was after he said that he fancied these for lunch at the nearby Gulshan-e-Iran. He accompanied his statement of desire with a salacious gleam and the graphic action of cupped palms bouncing spherical objects.

STOPPED PRESS

In obsolescence, this machine continues to reach out to people – and more directly than it ever did when the lines of hot-metal type slid off it to record the next day's news.

On the 3rd floor of Mumbai's historic TOI building, as you step out of the lift or wait for it, an old linotype setting machine glows its welcome. It's a riveting piece of machinery. Most of today's staffers are too young to have known the heat, grime and frenzy of hot-metal days, but they gaze on it reverentially. So do visitors unfamiliar even with the computerized and digitized processes by which today's paper is set, made up and printed.

Neither group can resist the temptation to run tremulous fingers across the linotype setter's solid bank of keys, the levers and other archaic protrusions. There is no 'Do Not Touch' sign, so they can do it with impunity. This is why the high gloss on the machine may come from the ministrations of the housekeeping staff, but the glow comes from the bonding. In obsolescence, this machine continues to reach out to people – and more directly than it ever did when the lines of hot-metal type slid off it to record the next day's news.

DESPATCHES FROM THE BATTLE FRONTS

It was made possible only with the help of the group's arch enemy in Delhi, Hindustan Times.

On May 31, 2005, BCCL launched India's first compact paper, *Mumbai Mirror*. And, guess what? It was made possible only with the help of the group's arch enemy in Delhi, *Hindustan Times*. "They agreed to rent us their press; we had no printing capacity left in ours. Nobody, even inhouse, had believed that they would help our cause." Ravi Dhariwal, had reason to sound satisfied; he was the one who had worked at making the TOI stop obsessing about HT.

The collaboration was all the more incredible because just a couple of years earlier the TOI had come up with the audacious combo offer and direct booking in place of the old circulation driver of invitation price. Used first with TOI and NBT in Delhi in 2003, it created an uproar in an incredulous market. It added the unheard-of two lakh copies within a week to TOI's numbers. "HT was struck motionless, we just marched ahead," said the strategist.

DESPATCHES FROM THE BATTLEFRONTS

The Mirror, like the starting – or closing – of all TOI publications, was part of Samir Jain's flotilla strategy, by which all moves are designed to protect the mother ship. It was most visibly deployed when The Independent was launched to knock the wind out of the Indian Post started by Vijaypat Singhania of the JK group.

Despite the shock waves it caused, as much within the Mumbai TOI's historic ramparts, this battle turned out to be a game of toy soldiers compared to the double-edged challenge mounted in 2005 by HT coming to Mumbai and the new DNA being launched by the cash-rich, Hindi-heartland Dainik Bhaskar group. Both wanted to grab a fat slice the country's most lucrative advertising market.

The TOI once again girded its loins – and tightened its bustier – pulling out all the stops, editorial and managerial, using every trick in the book and out of the box to stave off the threats to its monopolistic fortress. It has remained way ahead in both advertising revenue and circulation.

It was pouring with rain the day the DNA was finally launched. They had created a huge list of addresses, but the vendors refused to deliver saying the places were non-existent. There were indeed lots of mistakes in the database. But the TOI bastion remained undented as much by design as by default. It had been perfecting its defences for the past 167 years.

"HT was struck motionless, we just marched ahead," said the strategist.

It wasn't just about Mumbai and Delhi. India's changing and growing cities accelerated the onward march of the TOI from 2006 onwards. Circulation snowballed as the new editions started there took it upon themselves to guide the change and lead the growth; in this they were following the template designed in Bangalore a whole decade earlier. Now, with Jaideep Bose at the editorial helm, Pune, Nagpur and then Chennai all acquired editions of their own.

DESPATCHES FROM THE BATTLEFRONTS

Chennai picked up 2.5 lakh copies in just months. It was the Mumbai story in reverse. *The Hindu* was the entrenched ruler there and the TOI was the challenger. Again, as in Bangalore, where Deccan Herald had held sway, the TOI brought in its trade-mark contemporary, cosmopolitan attitudes, making the seemingly invincible old guard look jaded, faded and provincial.

As Ravi Dhariwal, put it, "Chennai was marching into modernity. Hoary old shops were replaced by sleek retail outlets. When I used to go there during my Unilever days, you could hardly see trousers on the street. Now you could barely spot a 'veshti'. We aimed at capturing the change." And it was captured brilliantly, even in the launch advertisement centred on a catchy jingle, 'Nakka Mukka', which won a Cannes Lion in 2009.

SMOKE GETS IN YOUR HI'S

People were forced to leave spacious departmental floors and stagger, craving for their kick, into the back lanes and hidden nooks. Here they discovered each other, lighting each other cigarettes, and igniting bonds with people they hardly knew existed even though they had worked in the same building for decades.

When smoking was officially banned in offices and public spaces in 2006, it lit up a never-before-known camaraderie. Call it the Nicotine Network. People were forced to leave spacious departmental floors and stagger, craving for their kick, into the back lanes and hidden nooks. Here they discovered each other, lighting each other cigarettes, and igniting bonds with people they hardly knew existed even though they had worked in the same building for decades.

SMOKE GETS IN YOUR HI'S

In Delhi, the exiled smokers also began appreciating the winter sunlight dappling the graves of the nearby Muslim cemetery. And the range of street food disbursed along the service lane of B'shah Zafar Marg, from summer fruit chaat to winter moongphali to the chana in tilted handis of burnished brass. It opened up a much wider world than the tried and tasted Mani's canteen.

Old divisions go up in smoke, gossip is passed around like a cigarette, and conviviality spreads between groups who otherwise had no opportunity to interact.

Else, the Stub Club discovered the disused passageways that took them to the terrace of Times House from where they savoured the view of patli gulleys and mohalla rooftops along with the long drags on their discredited cigarettes.

In Mumbai's many-crannied building, the back-staircase landings are now always littered with clandestine butts, and the steps are parked with an assortment of inter-department butts. Old divisions go up in smoke, gossip is passed around like a cigarette, and conviviality spreads between groups who otherwise had no opportunity to interact.

Yes, across BCCL's departments and centres, Anbumani Ramadoss as Health Minister had succeeded where scores of elaborate HR exercises had fallen by the wayside.

*"Either you got business
or you got dinner."
This was what Osho,
in another context,
had labelled
'a choiceless choice'.*

FALL OF THE WALL

The Editorial vs Management barrier was entrenched from Day Dot in newspaper offices across the world. The TOI did not go to the extremes of a legendary US paper where the lifts were programmed so that the one headed for the editorial floors would not stop on the management ones, and vice versa to prevent a confrontation of the primeval 'enemies'. And in the smoke-filled salons where editors gathered, they told superciliously of how 'No management type could enter the newsroom without being in serious danger of being shot at or spat at.'

In the early 1980s, TOI's advertising executives would go abroad to 'sell' the idea of its newly launched international supplements to countries with trade or other connections. An editorial person would go along to write the features, and use his embassy or consular links back home to get a foot in the door. The allowance was $75 a day, so as Guha put it "Either you got business or you got dinner." This was what Osho, in another context, had labelled 'a choiceless choice'.

These trips added another set of bricks to The Wall between Editorial and Management. Years later, after the latter had replaced the former as cock of the walk, a senior Response executive recalled in unforgiving detail how "In those days, we would be struggling with our briefcases and overcoats on public transport, managing with a measly sandwich, while the editorial person thanks to his contacts would be wined, dined, and chauffeured to his interviews." Setting her jaw in gloat mode, she added, "Well, it's different now, isn't it?"

When the LA Times brought down The Wall in the late 1990s, it devoted an entire section to this historic milestone. But the TOI had done it a decade earlier, with the arrival on the scene of the young Samir Jain who had little time and less inclination to pander to the elaborate mystique that editorial had conventionally built around itself.

Icons tumbled from their pedestals, the revenue-earning departments became the new stars. Over the years, editorial learnt to genuflect to the bottom-line; management valued the intellectual equity of editorial; and the hierarchies settled into an easy and more even relationship.

MEDIA'S LEADING LITE

By Bachi Karkaria

Not so long ago, morning newspapers looked and sounded like Winston Churchill. Now, morning newspapers look and sound like Kylie Minogue.

So, even though my daily broadsheet had been steadily becoming more about broads between the sheets, I still fell as flat as an old flatbed printing machine when its new avatar slipped under my door with the coquetry of a starlet slipping under the covers.

I called up one of the head honchos of the TOI. I assumed he was one of the prime movers of the paper's new look since he's from marketing, the discipline which has changed our entire culture from cellulite to sell you lite. Considering that he's the ultimate driving machine, he's sometimes referred to as the BMW.

This is apt also because he's a Bengali marketing whiz. "Good-morning, Boss," I said. "Nice to see the paper looking 'slimmer, slicker, sexier'." "Yes," he replied, "we've patented this thrillogy. First we made Femina look like a Femina Miss India. Now we've made the main paper look like our Page Three babes."

I countered, "Surely, there's a huge difference between a toy-boy and the TOI-Lady? With a drastic regimen, a stud might achieve a 27-and-a-half-inch waistline, but a 27-and-a-half-inch web, as the new width is known, sounds like an impossible makeover for a 163-year-old newspaper?"

The BMW purred in response, "Anjali Mukherjee was here." I decided not to mention the fact that the 'leader' had lost the first-mover advantage. The Hindustan Times, *followed by The* Sunday Indian Express, *had switched to the new 'international' seven-column format much earlier. I had another, more direct concern.*

Since I now belong to the tabloid world, I was seriously worried about our conventional space being colonised by the once-sedate broadsheet press. The insidious creation of the 'broadloid' had been going on for long, but the new look has made it as frontal as the Mid-Day *Mate. Every single day since the changed design, the masthead of my morning paper had been flanked by a blonde and a beefy footballer, both international. Did this mean that the print media simply can't do without foreign investment?*

While I debated over bringing up these matters of long-term policy, the BMW graciously said, "Come over for lunch some time in our sleek new dining room. Our executive chef now offers a daily choice of three menus: saatvik, slimming, and starving." So I chickened out of raising such contentious issues.

Of course, you can't change your size if you haven't first changed your content. The new look would be as ludicrous as Mr Vajpayee deciding to switch to jeans without first going in for an entire foster body. The sleek, sexy design simply wouldn't work if the Front Page was still plodding along with the same old news of politicians, potholes and poverty. So I decided to call the Editor.

This isn't as straightforward as it sounds since the more our national print media streamlines its product, the more complicated it makes its upper echelons. So, if you want to speak to an editor, you have to choose between managing, executive, resident, etc. At the rate at which it's going, there could be seven of them, one for each column.

I knew which editor I wanted to speak to. She was international, sleek and slimline long before her paper was. "Have you had problems adjusting to the new format?" I asked. "Yes and no," she replied with the in-built ambivalence of an edit-writer.

"While, on the one hand, space has become sacred, on the other, Sacred Space has been relegated to the lower half of the edit page." This gave me the cue for my next question. "So will the frontal 'sexiness' of the front page mean unabashed tabloidism in content?" "Yes and no," she repeated. "I see," I said and hung up.

Finally, it was important to know whether the new look was restricted to the newspaper, or whether the entire organisation had gone in for similar rightsizing. I spoke to the Human Resources Director. Had his policies also been reformatted like the pages and printing machines? "Of course," he said. "All colleagues must switch to the 'slimmer, slicker, sexier' look. To date, only tummies were expected to be as flat as the org structure, but now anyone with hips wider than seven columns will be asked to shape up or ship out. It's the latest corporate indicator of being width-it."

— *Reprinted from* Mid-Day *in the* Sunday Times of India, *June 2, 2002*

When the paper switched to the sleeker, slimmer, more international 7-column format

III

other empires

"Symbols, they can be interpreted in so many ways that although the actual image is clear enough, the interpretation is infinitely blurred, a sort of enormous rainbow of every possible colour you could imagine."

– Diana Wynne Jones –

He [Khushwant Singh] hated clichés and pomposity as much as he did empty Scotch bottles, and junked all three with equal lack of ceremony.

AT THE WEEKLY, STRONGLY

Khushwant Singh presided over the Weekly right through the 1970s, saved it from its destiny as the dog-eared denizen of dentists' waiting rooms and turned it into a virile breaker of circulation records. In fact he took magazine journalism itself by the scruff of its neck and shook it up, establishing a reader-friendly formula that has now been appropriated by all newspapers and magazines, no patent fees paid. He hated clichés and pomposity as much as he did empty Scotch bottles, and junked all three with equal lack of ceremony.

The unkind, the uninformed and those unable to stomach his success sniffed superciliously that the Weekly's surge in circulation was due to nothing more than its profusion of blouseless Bastar belles. True, 'TQ', tit quotient, was a must-have in its pages, but to say something so manifestly stupid is to insult the intelligence of the over three lakh people who bought it every week, to say nothing of the eight times as many who read each copy.

He brought in topics that real people were interested in, and featured them in the language of real people – not Hari Prasad Chaurasia, but the lusty, feisty Shakila Bano Bhopali. He personally sat through the trial of the serial killer Raman Raghav, and wrote a compelling series of articles on that and the mind of the psychopath. He was a sociological trendspotter, the New Rich and the cult following of Osho became bestselling cover stories. Nothing, however, surpassed cricket which he got written about in exhaustive detail.

The magazine's success drew and was furthered by the big names of politics, science, sport and literature; they all wrote willingly for the Weekly, and his band of well-trained sub-editors translated their high funda and/or dense prose into ordinary English. If the subs so enthusiastically made the article completely comprehensive with the addition of boxes, it was mostly because they got paid extra for these.

The unkind, the uninformed and those unable to stomach his success sniffed superciliously that the Weekly's surge in circulation was due to nothing more than its profusion of blouseless Bastar belles.

Khushwant Singh was the first to figure out the emotional bond which glued individuals to their communities, and he used the same adhesive to get readers stuck to his magazine. He featured the myriad communities of India as cover stories, and their members were hooked for life to the Weekly. He was the first 'marketing editor' of respectable Indian journalism. Though conventional respectability was quite manifestly not an entity he cared much about. If he saw a holy cow, he slaughtered it, drooling into his sloppily dyed beard.

Khushwant was a highly successful novelist whom BCCL persuaded to come on board. His wooing had caused heartburn in the Weekly ("He may be a great writer, but what does he know of editing a magazine?"). This was largely because his appointment would dislodge one of their own, the assistant editor Subroto Banerjee. He had been made Acting Editor after the exit of AS Raman, a worthy whose stewardship was marked by cover photographs of himself bowing to sundry godmen.

AT THE WEEKLY, STRONGLY

But the scoffers turned into instant acolytes when the sardar began working his miracles, and more so by the non-hierarchical camaraderie he brought into the Weekly office. An aghast visitor said in all seriousness, "Khushwant, you are actually allowing subs to walk into your office, and even sit down there?" His practice of entrusting cover stories to raw juniors occasioned major consternation in a culture where only the over-ripe got bylines.

In fact he committed worse sacrilege. He took us trainees for lunch – to his favourite Irani restaurants, George and Cafêx in the Fort area – instead of cultivating the city's rich and famous. Why should he have bothered when he was both? But our uninvited seniors sourly dismissed us as the 'biryani brigade'.

The slur was directed as much at the boss for his choice of cheap joints. He even took the consuls-general he entertained to dives such as Coronation Durbar, dining under stars struggling against the exhaust fumes, on a terrace overlooking the grimy neon of the Grant Road bazaar. Then he and his guests would drive past the nearby 'cages' of Mumbai's notorious redlight district. Strictly as tourists, not customers.

*"He may be
a great writer,
but what does he know
of editing
a magazine?"*

Khushwant Singh was always telling nubile journalists at the Weekly never to say they worked 'under' him. Just as when writing promos for articles, we were never to say, 'Gauri Deshpande on Girish Karnad'.

AT THE WEEKLY, STRONGLY

His unconventional regime was established from the very first moment he walked into the Weekly with his trade-mark plod. It was 8.45 am, 45 minutes before 'office time'. The surly Manohar was dusting the furniture when he saw this unkempt man in toweling T-shirt, sloppy trousers and sandals amble in. Mumbling to himself that the sardar invasion had arrived even before the sardarji, he brusquely told him in Marathi-Hindi, "Naya editor office nahin ayela hai." To which Khushwant Singh matter-of-factly replied, "Mein hi naya editor hoon."

He had made shabbiness his sartorial style and set his own social norms. He sent the Malabar Hill-ki-mynah hostesses into a twittering tizzy by arriving at their door at 8 pm and demanding dinner by nine, even if hardly any of the other guests had shown up. He didn't mind eating in the kitchen. He took along his own two pegs of whiskey to parties where he wasn't sure of getting the real McScotch.

"Naya editor office nahin ayela hai." To which Khushwant Singh matter-of-factly replied, "Mein hi naya editor hoon."

Khushwant Singh had left his bungalow-sized flat in south Delhi's Sujan Singh Park (built by and named after his wealthy contractor grandfather) to take over as the editor of the Mumbai-based weekly. Before he rented a flat in an appropriately seedy lane off Colaba Causeway, he lived as a paying guest in one of the spacious apartments overlooking the Oval Maidan and beyond it the Gothic high court and university.

He expected his own guests to show up sharp at the given time of 7 pm, and growled, 'You are late!' if you missed it by anything over three minutes. He offered you two drinks and then you left, or went out for dinner if that was part of the invitation. He, as unceremoniously, evicted even the most exalted guests from his Delhi house, originally by 10 pm, but now by 8.

The clock-watching wasn't so much bad hospitality as strict discipline. He rose at 4.45 am to work, writing his columns, articles or fiction in trade-mark, A3-sized, black-bound and ruled notebooks ordered from abroad. These were his manuscripts and would be worth a fortune for his heirs. He carried them (along with *The Times*, London, for the crossword) in a scuffed briefcase to the office, and the notebooks would be on the desk of his secretary Swami before the latter had briskly walked across from VT station and taken the lift up to the 4th floor.

The clock-watching wasn't so much bad hospitality as strict discipline.

The likes of Ali Sardar Jafri and Kaifi Azmi dropped into the office regularly as did an assortment of luminaries from other fields. Naturally there was no shortage of 'comely lasses', to use his phrase, in the ambit of the man with the self-publicized glad eye. Mumbai socialites with literary pretensions or merely those wanting him as a trophy guest to glitter up their parties, Ellora-sculpted dancers usually in the tow of the effusively gesticulating dance historian Sunil Kothari, bohemian artists clanking with tribal jewelry, and art critics in a more sober edition of ethnic chic were all part of the motley crowd of visitors.

Qurratulain 'Annie' Hyder, the iconic Urdu novelist, Sahitya Akademi award-winner (and later graced with the Jnanpith and the Padma Bhushan), had been appointed assistant editor shortly before Khushwant Singh took over. She was as indifferently dressed as the Sardar, but otherwise the two were complete opposites.

He was the quintessential 'dirty old man'; she was the spinster from a background of Lakhnavi purdah and convent primness. Their clashes rose from their separate causes, Palestine (hers) and Israel (his). Flinging the short pallu of her unstarched cotton sari over her shoulder like a spear, Annie would shoot out of her chair, shouting 'Mister Khushwant Singh!' even before she reached the closed door of his cabin. Pushing it open, she began hectoring the man on whatever seemingly pro-Jewish or anti-Arab comment he may have made in his piece. He submitted to her barrage helplessly.

AT THE WEEKLY, STRONGLY

But while she could slay Khushwant Singh with a single barb in this running battle, Annie, as she was known to her colleagues and friends, disintegrated in embarrassment over the scatological comments of a then eight-year-old Fareed Zakaria, who often came after school to pick up his mother, Fatma. On one occasion, she actually fled from her desk in shock when the boy drew a pair of breasts and labelled them 'honey bags'.

Annie's pieces – and her presence – provided much of the weightiness of the Weekly. She would write her articles in Urdu, and then translate them into English; at the end of the day, she would be ankle-deep in crumpled drafts.

But for all her intellectual stature, Annie could be down to earth, or even as skittish as a schoolgirl. Once, apropos of nothing, she declared, "You know, the Queen (of England) looks so dowdy because she wears the wrong kind of bra."

One so-called winter day in Mumbai, she arrived at the office wearing a huge, black and rather mouldy overcoat. "It's from Harrod's" she said, as if that justified such excessive cover up. But then she also never stepped out in the afternoon without covering her dyed black hair with her pallu and a faded black umbrella, plus large dark glasses. It was merely the sun, not her celebrity status that called for such elaborate precautions.

She gave us trainees far more quarter than she accorded to her lofty peers, and responded to our cheeky temerities with a sardonic arch of her pencilled eyebrows. She once theatrically despaired over the hash that Parsis had made of their exquisite Persian names: "Jehangir ko bana diya hai Jingoo; Behman ko bana diya hai Bomi; Faridun ko bana diya hai Freddie. Lahaul willa quwwat!"

It was merely the sun, not her [Qurratulain Hyder] celebrity status that called for such elaborate precautions.

Khushwant Singh's informality suffused the Weekly hall with a bonhomie quite unknown in the neighbouring magazines and certainly not evident in the stiff newsrooms of the dailies.

At lunch-time, no one went to the canteen whose cooking aromas would start wafting two floors down one hour earlier. The assistant editor, R Gopalkrishna ('RGK'), went out to pick up more Charminars from the corner shop. SV Vasudev nipped out for a quick drink, as did Benedict Costa who included 'kabb-babs' in the ritual. Jal Engineer sat at his chief-sub's table, presiding over his full lunch brought from home by Rosie, who dutifully stood by like an aide de camp throughout.

The Weekly women ate together at conjoined office desks laid out with the instruments of appeasement: Elizabeth Rao's compact American lunch-pail with lavish leftovers, Fatma Zakaria's hotcase of fresh kormas delivered steaming by her Man Friday, Pascal, assorted tiffin boxes of varied culinary skills – and Annie's two dented aluminium dabba-sections always containing dry rotis and congealed mutton chops.

Her colourful eccentricities more than made up for the drab and predictable contents of her lunchbox. Besides, as the resident intellectual she was expected to provide only food for thought,

AT THE WEEKLY, STRONGLY

and not deign to descend to mundane domesticities. But she could gamely dumb-down, and so, one afternoon, Annie launched into an anthology of limericks on our Weekly colleagues, culminating in the most memorable one on Ben Costa.

A dashing young Goan named Costa,
In his heart amorous longings did fosta.
He wooed a young lass
On the way to High Mass,
But on the way back from Communion,
He losta.

R Gopalkrishna and Jal Engineer were the odd couple of the Weekly. 'RGK' was learned in Sanskrit, steeped in the classics, South Indian, chauvinistic and taciturn. 'Engine' was garrulous, over-meticulous, Parsi, announced his name in slow deliberate syllables on the telephone, and often displayed the symptoms of a menopausal male especially when making us stay behind till the last comma was in place.

RGK always wore dark trousers, white bush shirt and chappals: the first time he bought shoes was when Khushwant Singh sent him on a junket to Germany. He came away half way through the trip complaining of the 'curd which smelled', and 'the aggressive look of the cattle in the pastures; not like our beautiful docile Indian cows'. Like most Parsis of his generation, Jal Engineer's uniform was starched white bush shirt and white duck trousers which he hitched up with his elbows in a compulsive gesture.

Engineer and RGK sat at adjacent desks facing the mass of sub-editors. Jal would irritate RGK with the most inane of queries, especially galling to a man who inhabited another stratosphere. This encounter was typical. Jal turns to RGK and says in that slow, deliberate drawl, "Go-pal where is the Everest Advertising Agency?" Gopal, inwardly seething at such a mundane, even ridiculous query, keeps looking straight ahead, puffs harder on his Charminar, and replies through clenched teeth, "I suppose it is in the Himalaya."

AT THE WEEKLY, STRONGLY

SV Vasudev was another of the Weekly characters. He alternated his free time between the race course and the city's speakeasies. In his desk drawer, he kept a lined school exercise book in which he would constantly scribble intricate calculations on the weight of the jockey, of the saddle, etc to work out a winning formula. He too was taciturn. Once, a young sub was throwing one of her tantrums because she had lost some copy she had laboriously edited, and had spluttered, "This is the last straw!" Vasu, who occupied the adjoining desk, said quietly, "I did not know you were a camel."

Pritish Nandy was as sartorially flashy as Khushwant was sloppy, given to all-black outfits, unbuttoned shirts and tight jeans. He was a sort of bald Rasputin.

NANDY, THE RAGING BULL

After the interim of the vanilla MV Kamath, the Weekly got another celebrity editor. Pritish Nandy was as sartorially flashy as Khushwant was sloppy, given to all-black outfits, unbuttoned shirts and tight jeans. He was a sort of bald Rasputin. He was also a poet, fastidious about the language. He was known to spot a mistake on a page at 20 paces. He introduced edgy design to the Weekly, and promoted upcoming artists (and, it was murmured, his own art collection).

Unlike Khushwant Singh, he was part of the innermost circle of the Jains, notably Samir and Nandita. He was as much impresario as editor. He actually looked the part. You could almost see him in top hat and velvet cape, cracking a whip – in his case it would have had sequins winking at its tip. But even if these were metaphorical, the boots were de rigeur for him on a daily basis.

Pritish Nandy once stormed into the office, breathing fire, and with a copy of the Weekly rolled under his arm. At the time it was in its brief broadsheet avatar.

NANDY, THE RAGING BULL

He summoned the four assistant editors into his room brandished the copy wildly, and launched into a torrent of abuse. He thundered, "I saw this on the flight, I hung my head in shame. I couldn't look my fellow passengers in the eye. It's a f…ing disgrace. What kind of boring s…t have you produced?" Then, before the aghast journos' eyes, Nandy proceeded to tear the paper into shreds, fling them on his carpet, and stamp vigorously on the pieces with his trade-mark boots. As always, in half an hour, Nandy was back to his ebullient self.

"I learnt more with Mr Nandy than any other editor." Coming from Sherna Gandhy, one of the country's most efficient journalists, this is indeed stratospheric praise.

Sherna, who was chief sub and assistant editor throughout the Pritish years, continued, "One comma wrongly placed or missing and he'd come out and bellow, and the whole fourth floor would hear about it. Once while he was away in the States, an issue appeared with several typos in one feature. 'Thank your stars Nandy is not here,' I had murmured to the sub who had handled it, little realising that (in the days before e-papers) copies were air-mailed to him wherever he was. Sure enough he was on the phone, and started the diatribe. The erring sub was harangued for 15 minutes long distance. We watched his face getting smaller and smaller."

Saroj Nagi used to work in the Weekly's Delhi bureau. She had heard of his temper tantrums and war dances on layout sheets which did not meet with his artistic approval. However, when he came to Delhi he was usually preoccupied with Maneka Gandhi and other affairs of state, so he

Pritish Nandy once stormed into the office, breathing fire, and with a copy of the Weekly rolled under his arm. At the time it was in its brief broadsheet avatar.

didn't normally come to the bureau office. One day, however he did, and as usual something or the other lit his temperamental fuse. Saroj stood paralysed in shock as he ranted. "Every second word was a gaali. I could not believe that this was the same man who wrote the sensitive poetry I had so admired."

NANDY, THE RAGING BULL

Sherna added, "To be fair to him, Nandy gamely accepted criticism of himself. He had written a lengthy intro to a Jayalalitha cover story which I considered extremely sexist, making offensive references to her weight. I went into his cabin and I was so upset that I blurted out my objections in front of his guests, an American writer and wife. Nandy listened quietly and said he would change it. When the couple came out, the woman patted me on the shoulder and said, 'You were right', but I realised that I should have waited till they had left. Mr Nandy however did not give even the slightest hint of annoyance, and did indeed excise the personal remarks."

He also prided himself on being the rare editor who acknowledged the importance of the Desk. He'd say, "Writers are a dime a dozen; I spit on them. The real stars are the subs who turn around the copy and make it sparkle."

And his unorthodox advice to both writers and sub-editors was: "You must break the hymen of the story."

"Every second word was a gaali. I could not believe that this was the same man who wrote the sensitive poetry I had so admired."

Like his celebrated pre-predecessor, he was a ladies man, but unlike Khushwant Singh, actually acted upon his braggadocio. One of the enduring stories was how a TV starlet, whom he had dumped as determinedly as he had pursued, landed up at the office, fumed into his secretary's room, and demanding to see him. The seasoned Maria pretended that her boss was out, but the lady refused to budge. The secretary, however, was a practised hand at deflection, and managed to alert Nandy in the adjacent room. He slipped out of the door, RAN down the corridor and bounded up one floor to the *Independent* which he also edited.

"Writers are a dime a dozen; I spit on them. The real stars are the subs who turn around the copy and make it sparkle."

Some-time *Science Today* editor Mukul Sharma had acted in *Paroma*, an edgy film made by his ex-wife, the well-known actress-turned-director Aparna Sen. He played the foreign-returned photographer who had an affair with his subject, a traditional Bengali housewife. The beauteous Rakhee essayed the title role. Mukul boasted to his friend Pritish that when he lay atop her for a bedroom shot, he counted 29 golden flecks in her amber eyes. Nandy smirked and said, "36".

Many admirers of Nandy's journalistic skills criticised his friendship with Maneka Gandhi. They accused her of "turning him into a political animal who fancied himself as a kingmaker. This was his undoing."

The Weekly under Pritish became more controversial than it had ever been. The editor ran one gob-smacking story after another, a loose cannon firing at the powerful and pompous. JB Patnaik, the Chief Minister of Orissa, was only one of his targets. The magazine ran a cover story alleging that anyone who sought protection or a job from him would be expected to provide sexual favours, irrespective of whether they were men or women. Patnaik lodged 36 cases against Nandy and the Weekly. Orissa magistrates refused to accept the company's affidavits, finally only one was brave enough to agree. Nandy's lieutenant, Sailesh Kottary, seemed to have no job other than to traverse the country juggling all the court cases centring on his flamboyant boss.

Ostensibly, the Patnaik cases were for something else. The controversial issue had also

NANDY, THE RAGING BULL

featured four double spreads of nudes by celebrity photographer Prabhuda Das Gupta. The very correct Sherna had objected. Pritish held his ground on the classical it's-art-not-pornography argument. But his assistant editor was vindicated. This photo-spread provided the Orissa government a legitimate excuse to ban the issue from the state. It cited the 'obscenity' of these nudes, the perfect fig leaf for the real reason for the ban – the omnivorous sexual appetite of the Chief Minister.

Nandy actually had to get police protection when an outraged Chandraswami, the controversial godman, took out a 'supari' (the humble betel nut was the Mumbai underworld's code word for a contract killing) against him. He had tried to prevent publication of a Weekly cover story that he had gone around the world cheating half a dozen heads of state with cheap streetside magician's tricks, and had run away with millions worth of diamonds. Nandy was threatened from London by the 'godman's' powerful friend, Adnan Khashoggi, the billionaire Turkish-Saudi Arabian arms-dealer and businessman. But the Weekly cover story was cited in several cases later instituted against Chandraswami.

Naturally, he refused to grant Nandy the interview that he sought. So the journo resorted to subterfuge, a sort-of sting. He enlisted Rajat Sharma who was then *Onlooker* editor. Nandy recalled: "I pretended to be his chamcha, and a moronic side-kick at that. I fawningly asked Chandraswami if I could get a photograph with him. He then suddenly said, 'Yeh Pritish Nandy kaun hai? Haramzada hamare peechhey laga hai.' (This b….d is after my blood.) We replied 'He's a rascal, a badmash!' Chandraswami said, 'I will give a million dollars if you can stop him writing about me. You pay him off and you can keep the rest.'

'I [Chandraswami] will give a million dollars if you can stop him writing about me. You [Pritish Nandy] pay him off and you can keep the rest.'

"Then, I piped up, 'Guruji, ek baat bolu? What if I am this Pritish Nandy?' The godman used an expletive and said, 'Dekho, yeh hai meri teesri aankh. Mein bhavishya dekh sakta hoon. Humko koi ullu nahin bana sakta hai.' (I can see the future with my third eye. No one can make a fool of me). So I asked him, 'What is my future then?' Chandraswami condescendingly replied 'Capability hai. You aren't as much of an ass as you appear to be. You will get somewhere.' "

NANDY, THE RAGING BULL

Nandy's explosive, but painstakingly researched interviews were a signature of his Weekly. The one with President Giani Zail Singh, in which he complained, 'No one is keeping me informed' led to a constitutional crisis.

The controversial cover stories called for unconventional methods of news gathering. Charles Sobhraj had written a novel from jail. According to Nandy, this international criminal was in love with his lawyer. We 'managed' this girl friend, and got a Xerox of the novel, and published an extract.

Similar tactics were deployed to get a detailed story on Bangladeshi President Zia ur Rehman's corruption. These were revealed to Nandy by his mistress whom he again managed to prise open. She was tucked away in New York with his cache. Why did she confide in Nandy? He shrugged, "May be I was the first man who was not interested in her pile of cash."

Nandy's provocative style was stamped across all the Weekly's covers. Amitabh Bachchan had a series of flops, but the industry was in denial. The line across the cover blazed, 'Superstar: Finished!' Another said, 'Is Sunil Gavaskar the worst captain in the world?' Guess who wrote that cover story? Shashi Tharoor. He was already climbing through the ranks at the UN, but Nandy had "known him in Cal and I tapped into these old contacts and built on my network".

My [Ashok Jain] mandate was
to freshen the whole group,
not just the magazines.
But I found it impossible
to talk to the senior journalists
of the Times of India.
They were old fogeys who
thought they owned the world.

CLASH OF THE TITANS

The story of Pritish Nandy coming on board BCCL started literally on board. That of a plane from Bombay to Calcutta. The flashy 30-something had worked with MJ Akbar, the original *enfant terrible* of Indian journalism who had displayed his brash arrogance even as a *Times of India* trainee in the early 1970s.

Nandy had just been awarded a Bhabha fellowship to write a historical novel based on Vasco da Gama's journey from Lisbon to Calicut, and was on a flight back to Calcutta. Ashok Jain was in the seat next to him, and before the landing announcement crackled, he had invited Nandy "to have breakfast at home with me." Asked where, the distinguished gentleman had told him, "When you look out of your flat in Sonali Apartments, you see a lawn, don't you? Well, I live in the bungalow attached to it." Nandy went over to Jain's House in Alipore, was offered a job, and was so swept off his feet that he slashed his moorings in Kolkata, jettisoned his Fellowship, and agreed to join almost the very next day.

CLASH OF THE TITANS

As he told it,"My mandate was to freshen the whole group, not just the magazines. But I found it impossible to talk to the senior journalists of the *Times of India*. They were old fogeys who thought they owned the world. They were constantly throwing their power and influence at me. Giri treated his post like a feudal legacy. I was constantly being told, 'Giri said this to the PM'. 'Mrs G asked Giri for advice on that'. But as I saw it, the job of the *Times of India*'s editor was not to advise the PM. His job was to stand up and tell his readers where the PM was going wrong."

Here we witness one of the many grand clashes of the Times of India building, the figurative clang of steel so loud that it reverberated right across the road and ricocheted off the vaulted dome of Victoria Terminus. No eyebrows need be raised, no askance looked. This is the stuff of all legendary organisations.

Giri, for his part, had reportedly told Ashok Jain, that "Pritish Nandy can't even write English. He writes incomplete sentences. He writes advertising English." When he heard about this, the novelist-poet Pritish spat out, "I write as I speak, not all his pompous grandstanding stuff. I'd be ashamed if I wrote like Giri."

The big showdown came just before the sesquicentennial, when the Jains wanted newer minds to bring in the freshness desperately needed to shed the 'Old Lady' image. Nandy's name was suggested as Managing Editor of the *Times of India*. What ensued was, in his version, 'power play, not so much power struggle'. A list of people to be 'invited to join' was drawn up. By whom? Depends on who's telling the story. Pritish Nandy, Gautam Adhikari, Dileep Padgaonkar all claimed to be the Master Listmaker, each relegating the others to the role of 'advisers or merely executors.'

Nandy said that right from the start of his inning at BCCL he could cut a swathe across the mandarins of the group "out of sheer arrogance, because I had the backing of Ashok Jain. He was the reason I was there. I was an unstated first among equals, given the freedom to bring in change, even though I was vastly outnumbered by the bureaucracy led by Dr Tarneja and Krishnamurthy.

On Pritish's first day at the office, the debonair, safari-suited Dr T had complained, "He has come to work in torn jeans, and a shirt open showing half of his chest. He will destroy the culture of the place. Has he come dressed for a street fight?"

On Pritish's first day at the office, the debonair, safari-suited Dr T had complained, "He has come to work in torn jeans, and a shirt open showing half of his chest. He will destroy the culture of the place. Has he come dressed for a street fight?"

Portentous words. Some weeks later, Nandy had an encounter with PR Krishnamurthy, keeper of the keys – and the paper clips – to the kingdom, which you can read about in 'Dealing with PRK'.

"She stood on a pulpit and preached to Indian women what they should be."

VIVACIOUS VIMLA

Vimla Patil, the entrenched editor of *Femina*, had no great love for Pritish Nandy when he began stomping over her domain as publishing director. Pritish returned the compliment, and then some more. According to him, "She stood on a pulpit and preached to Indian women what they should be. I had serious reservations about this. I didn't think that's what a magazine for contemporary women should be."

It is noteworthy that Vimla had assiduously stuck to Mrs Patil, and refused to use the Ms that her younger colleagues wore like a bra-less banner in the first flush of '70s feminism. It's another matter that in India, Ms has come to replace only Miss and not become the marital status-neutral label it was coined to be. Under other editors and publishing directors, *Femina* would get as edgy as a sharply cut business suit, and as feminine as lip gloss. It would move from its base line of a Woman of Substance to Gen W and then to 'I Believe'.

Vimla Patil was so stunning in her younger days as assistant editor of Femina that, when she went through the managerial hall on her way to the Lunch Room or to meet her mentor, Dr Tarneja, everybody just put down their pens and unabashedly ogled. But then those were more sexist times.

And another Mrs Patil story, this one told by Darryl D'Monte. "Vimla was all ready to publish a eulogy of Indira Gandhi as soon as Emergency was declared. We were aghast and we finally persuaded her to recall the article which had already been sent for production. We gave her the fake warning that under the new censorship rules, no publication was allowed to mention Mrs Gandhi's name without prior permission."

Femina *would get as edgy as a sharply cut business suit, and as feminine as lip gloss. It would move from its base line of a Woman of Substance to Gen W and then to 'I Believe'.*

But Mrs Patil was a smart cookie who had held her own in a then extremely male chauvinist organisation, and if she 'fell' for the ploy, it was only because she herself chose to do so.

PUFFY & SNUFFY

"Why I [Mr Krishnan] should stop? You [feminist young women of Femina*] go puff-puff, and I go snuff-snuff."*

Femina had a clerk addicted to his snuff box. Okay, to each his own. But instead of keeping his fix to himself, he would stop by each of the editorial desks, take a huge sniff, sneeze loudly, and not entirely into his handkerchief. In fact most times he didn't pull out the stained rag fast enough. The women suspected this was deliberately designed to annoy them. None more so than the drop-dead gorgeous Prabha Kripal Singh whose delicate nose trembled and whose delectable bunny teeth gritted each time Krishnan went into his routine at her table. "Please Mr Krishnan, don't do that. Please stop this snuff of yours," she said in her chi-chi tone.

But Mr Krishnan had his own grouse and his own riposte. The Tam Brahm was equally offended by the smoking habits of the feminist young women of *Femina*. So when Prabha pulled him up, he pulled himself up to his full height of five feet three and said, "Why I should stop? You go puff-puff, and I go snuff-snuff."

"Please Mr Krishnan,
don't do that.
Please stop this snuff of yours,"

THE CURIOUS CASE OF SAROSH BANAJI

In his spare time, he was a crack shot on the rifle range.

Sarosh Banaji was a strange elf-like sub at *Filmfare*, as pale as if he had spent his whole life under a sunless rock. He was also a difficult employee, but because he was on the Wage Board not on contract, he could not be sacked without a long process involving the industrial tribunal.

So the company chose the easier option. Banaji was simply given no work. He would sit at his desk staring wordlessly into space from 9.30 am to 5 pm, and then get up and leave as silently.

Shanta Gokhale, the feted Marathi writer who worked for many years at the TOI Group, described it with typical dry humour, "He walked out of the office as if he had just stepped out of a sewer, his hands stretched away from his body, his face puckered in disdain."

But there was a secret life to this colourless, odourless specimen. In his spare time, he was a crack shot on the rifle range. It's a surprise and a mercy that he did not bring his skills to the office he so despised.

It [the Metropolis] *lived up to its tag-line 'All Bombay is covered with MOS'.*

REIGN OF SAMRAT

In the early 1990s Samrat Publications was created to launch the group's new-look newspapers, The *Independent* and then the *Metropolis* on Saturday. The first appealed to the sophisticated reader, the latter became the country's first full-scale, city-centric broadsheet, with four sections to enable more colour pages than in any other paper. It lived up to its tag-line 'All Bombay is covered with MOS'.

Samrat's first brand manager was Chandni Sehgal. She looked and acted like the commander of a boot camp. Bharat Kumar Raut was editor and I had been subpoenaed from the TOI as consulting editor. So, I can authoritatively confess that several of the editorial innovations which established MOS as dynamically different emanated from Chandni.

REIGN OF SAMRAT

Soon Samrat became a media experimental theatre, smaller, nimbler and more risk-able than the huge TOI. Management orders to 'try out this', 'institute that' would be issued from above, which was actually two floors below. In those pre-'Satanic' Rushdie days, we had labeled these instructions 'fatwas'.

'With all these feathers, by now I [Fawzia Madni] should have flown right away!'

Here is the favourite Samrat war-room story of Fawzia Madni, who succeeded Chandni. "One afternoon, I came panting up from A-squared (that was Arun Arora, our director in charge) with yet another directive. I apologetically asked the consulting editor to carry out just 'this one last fatwa'. She threw a fit, and it was indeed well-near impossible to do what had been asked for in the time-frame given. But, I whined, 'Please, please, Batch,' adding, 'if we pull this off, it will really be one more feather in your cap.' To which she replied caustically, 'With all these feathers, by now I should have flown right away!' "

Then a strike struck Samrat. The cleaners were proactively dirtying the place. You would arrive to see batata vadas smashed on keyboards. Brand Manager Fawzia, in her disgust and naivete, told Mr Arora, "It's getting very difficult to work. I'm going to ring my mother and ask her to send our servant to clean up my room." Samrat's executive director paled, ordered her to do no such thing, and thus preempted having a bigger labour mess on his hands.

The Independent, having served its strategic purpose, was shut down in 1994, and *Bombay Times* rose from its ashes. But there were many editorial experiments before the phoenix could evolve into a sequined bird of paradise. In the early weeks, the BT editor and Bharat Kumar Raut were summoned to the boardroom to face a firing squad of top management telling them that the fledging paper was too tame.

Seeing the editor's manifest frustration, 'Nippy' Singh, the debonair head of RMD, chivalrously threw out a lifeline by saying, "But I suppose, you can't write about some holy cows." At which point the editor burst out: "Some? There's a whole tabela (cattle-shed) of them!"

REIGN OF SAMRAT

As Bharat loved to recall, "First there was a stunned silence. Then there was the noisy clatter of AK-47s falling to the floor." Before the guns, there were the long knives. A former editor of The Independent had gone over to the Ambanis when they were to start the Business and Political Observer (shortened to BPO, but no relation to the outsourcing which would stab jobs in the West much later). His former deputy was also to join, but he was still at Samrat. The traitor actually sat in his office offering 30% salary increases to staffers to persuade them to cross over. Things got so bad that every time the brand manager and editor returned to their rooms, they would find a resignation letter on their desks.

They managed to stave off the crisis, but it had come close to sudden death. They dubbed that period the 'Night of the Long Envelops.'

FINE PRINT

... 'going down for glass'.

When the giant rotary machines still thundered at the Times building on Mumbai's DN Road, photogravure was the production process. The paper would be transferred on film and put on glass sheets for a final check by editorial teams before being etched on the huge cylinders for printing. In the magazines, this weekly/fortnightly ritual was called 'going down for glass'.

Every newcomer at *Femina* had her well-waxed leg pulled on this account. She would be told it was her turn to 'Go down for glass', and her querulous look would be met with a straight face and the explanation: "Oh, Gravure always asks us for a glass of wine – or fresh juice if you prefer – when they are ready with their part of the process. Today it's your turn." The girl would refresh her lipstick and traipse down for the party only to have to end up needing glasses after that eye-straining process in the dark cavern.

The Gravure department had its legends. In the 1960s it was the large blond German Gnadig, who was an accomplished landscape painter. He was followed by the dark and stocky Goan, Robert Dango, as loud as the Teuton was taciturn.

The next production head, like Dango from the ranks, was the Nike-wearing, hard-talking, Purnendu Sen, a cynical, no-nonsense Bengali.

THE SENTINEL

If Sen was asked to do anything beyond his set parameters, he would say "Sahib, nahi hoga." Then he would emphatically intone, "Even Brahmma cannot do this."

Purnendu Sen was dubbed 'Prince of the Underworld' because of his uncompromising stand. He was the czar of the best-in-Asia Times Suburban Press in Kandivali ever since it was set up in 1987, but even as the Gravure Superintendent, he was Judgement Day itself. Not just for editorial but also for Response, which was then still Advertising.

Circulation sat further up the food chain as far as on-time delivery was concerned, but its honchos too were uncharacteristically restrained in their sabre-rattling with the unbending Purnendu. In any event, his tightly run ship was never the cause of schedule turbulence.

Even the all-powerful Dr Tarneja and his congenitally dismissive successor, P. R. Krishnamurthy, deferred to him.

If Sen was asked to do anything beyond his set parameters, he would say "Sahib, nahi hoga." Then he would emphatically intone, "Even Brahmma cannot do this."

But he did very occasionally show his softer side. He once inexplicably sent Niloufer Bilimoria of the Response department a gift. It was a penknife.

Only one sentence is needed to illustrate the terror in which the master printer was held. When Pradeep Guha went off to Kolkata to get married to Parpia in '81, he told his junior colleagues, "If Thiru, (their own tempestuous boss) and Purnendu call you at the same time, you have to answer Sen's summons first."

In those early days, Fawzia Madni, handling three of the group's four magazines as a lowly Advertising officer, felt his wrath the most. He would throw back the ad material that she had sent, saying "I can't accept this. The transparencies are scratched," or give some other finicky reason. She would have to go back to, say, Ishan Raina, who was then Accounts director at Lintas, and beg him to give a fresh lot. All this happening at deadline time would make Fawzia lose her curls.

"If Thiru, (their own tempestuous boss) and Purnendu call you at the same time, you have to answer Sen's summons first."

Which fast forwards us two floors up and 10 years later to when she was brand manager of TOI. One Saturday afternoon, Fawzia had gone for a haircut (it was after all her day off), when all hell broke loose. Purnendu was doing a tandava on the front page of the Sunday Review because the advertisement was elbowing into editorial. Someone had goofed on the size.

Editorial, battling its own deadlines, was in no mood to remake its part of the page. It would have capitulated soon enough because it was easier to cut an article than a pre-cast advertisement. But Purnendu Sen wanted someone's head, and that day, it was the half- shorn one of Ms Madni.

The Sunday Review editor used her diplomatic skills to placate him, and Fawzia ultimately did not have to haul herself back into town from her suburban salon with a lop-sided haircut. But

Purnendu had the last word. "I'm doing it only for you," he told the SR editor, "Not for that other long-nosed lady." The OLNL got to hear about this only another decade later, when we were swapping stories for this book.

THE SENTINEL

Sunil Rajshekhar was soft-spoken and civilised unlike the usual swashbucklers of Response. Once he, Purnendu and Niloufer landed up at Mainland China in Saki Naka after some TOI event in the burbs. Tanked up, Purnendu was in an expansive mood. He said in his usual hoarse drawl – and Bengali-Hindi, "Arrey, Sunil, yeh toh batao. Tumhara jaisa gentleman aadmi Times of India jaisa company mein itna bada kaise bana? (How did a gentleman like you manage to rise so high in a company like the TOI?")

DEALING WITH PRK

He [PR Krishnamurthy] rose from a secretary to become the omnipotent GM of Bombay office.

All organisations of a certain age have a PR Krishnamurthy. If they didn't, they would have to indent him. PRK had all the smug pompousness of the self-made man. He rose from a secretary to become the omnipotent GM of Bombay office, which for almost 150 years was the company's HQ. And like all self-made men, he dressed in a pristine white safari suit.

In the words of Pradeep Guha: "Till the end, he was someone not many people liked to interact with. But matters he knew, he knew very well and there was much to learn from him. What he didn't know but still expounded at length and with authority, you could simply ignore."

With his felicity for observation, RK Laxman said about the portly GM: 'His laugh ripples down from throat to tummy." While PRK wasn't usually given to humour, he unwittingly gave rise to it.

Computers had just entered the TOI and the seniormost had been bestowed these new status symbols. Krishnamurthy proudly told a visitor, "Look here, this is my computer, and this is its rat."

Maybe he never said it, and this was just another 'management' story from the editorial side of the trenches. But it must be told all the same.

DEALING WITH PRK

He was also the man who showed great concern for women staffers with no one to leave their small children with. As he put it, "We must install a crechie for them."

Niloufer Bilimoria of the exotic looks had joined Response from the Oberoi's corporate communications department. She was put in charge of 'International', with its two wings of global ads and international media representation. In pre-liberalised times this entailed a legal tight rope. So PG promptly sent her to meet PRK, who knew the complexities of the law better even than those of the perfect sambar.

When she entered his room, he didn't even deign to look at her. She timorously said, "I've come to ask you about a problem." Still refusing to make eye contact, he said imperiously, "I speak only to department heads." "But I am the department head," countered Niloufer bristling at such a sexist assumption. PRK didn't budge and kept his eyes on the papers in front of him. She flounced out, took her offence to her boss, who got on the phone with the great man. He grudgingly relented. But over time, he "became my pal, especially since I had to get his legal advice almost every week".

With his felicity for observation, RK Laxman said about the portly GM: 'His laugh ripples down from throat to tummy.'

Soon after he joined BCCL, Nandy, the raging bull, found his first red rag in PRK. This is how he described it.

"My wife and two small daughters had come by train to Bombay a week after I joined. I sent a bill for their tickets, which was simply not being reimbursed. We were living hand to mouth, and Bombay was an expensive city.

"I [Nandy] walked into Krishnamurthy's office and said, 'My bill seems to be stuck somewhere.' 'No,' he replied with that smug look of his, 'It's not stuck anywhere else. It is with me.'

"I walked into Krishnamurthy's office and said, 'My bill seems to be stuck somewhere.' 'No,' he replied with that smug look of his, 'It's not stuck anywhere else. It is with me.' 'Is there a problem?' I asked. 'Yes,' he said, 'how do I know they came by first class? Where is the proof?' I was flabbergasted, and informed him that tickets are taken away by the TC at the station's exit. He then said, 'How do I know you are not cheating the company – huh?'

"At this point, I lost it, and sprang on Krishnamurthy, saying menacingly, 'You think I'm cheating?' I held him by the collar of his white safari suit and said, 'I will kick your teeth in if you dare to suggest that I got my wife and kids in Third Class to cheat the company? Do you think I'm your father's servant?' I then stormed out. The bill was settled the next day. And Krishnamurthy was sugar and honey with me forever after."

This admittedly is a one-sided, biased version which would never have got past the exacting editorial standards of Pritish Nandy. Forgive me, your chronicler did not even try to get PRK's corroboration of this close encounter of the 'Third Class' kind.

At a Filmfare Awards function, the MC, Amin Sayani, quipped, "When Mr [PK] Roy returns from a long lunch, a murmur goes through the great hall of the 3rd floor administrative office, 'Peekay aaya hai'."

GMs PAST

PK Roy was the general manager from the late 1960s to the early '70s. At a Filmfare Awards function, the MC, Amin Sayani, quipped, "When Mr Roy returns from a long lunch, a murmur goes through the great hall of the 3rd floor administrative office, 'Peekay aaya hai'."

JC Jain was among the most powerful GMs of the time when this was the top executive position. He had a reedy voice, sometimes cruelly described as 'having one vocal chord'. The story goes that on a visit to Hollywood, JC met the smokey-voiced beauty, Lauren Bacall. Trying to think of something smart to say to this icon, he quipped, "Miss Bacall, is it true that you are sometimes mistaken for a man?" The lady arched her famous eyebrows and retorted, "No. Are you?"

The fixer was a critical species of the corporate ecosystem, able to insinuate his way through the corridors of power.

THE FIXER

In less-liberalised times, the fixer was a critical species of the corporate ecosystem, able to insinuate his way through the corridors of power. He had to be a smooth talker. Narendranath Swamy, in the Bangalore office, could do so in many tongues. He was always dressed in coloured kurta and white Aligarhis, glasses dangling from a black cord. He had an excellent memory for names, and dropped them with aplomb.

He claimed he could speed up – or slow down – anything, and had a manifest familiarity with politicians. The branch used him more to access the secretaries of various departments to procure government advertising.

Sunil Rajshekhar, the branch head, and KR Ramesh, the Response manager, would go along with him to the Karnataka state assembly. They would walk past the peons sitting self-importantly outside the cabins of their 'Saar'. Trotting ahead, Naren would greet each one by name, and, turning back, imperiously say, 'Sunil, give him a tenner'; 'Ramesh, give him a tenner.'

On each visit the two managers would have been divested of at least a hundred bucks, non-chargeable to company account.

THE FIXER

Once during the tenure of Veerappa Moily, the trio went to the Vidhan Soudha for some other work, and Swamy said, "Since we are here, let's drop in on the CM." Narendra breezed into his office with a cheery 'Namaskaram' to the PA. Visibly annoyed by this unannounced intrusion, Moily said, "What can I do for you Naren? But as you can see I am in a meeting." Unfazed, Swamy replied, "Yes, yes, Sir, we have just come to say hello." And doing just that, he left, with an embarrassed Sunil and Ramesh hurrying out behind him.

As with all self-proclaimed fixers, it was always a moot point as to how many tasks got done due to his influence, and how many had been effected merely 'in due course'.

Loo-NATIC ASYLUM

It [Mumbai's executive men's toilet] historic in its own way because it was the only common ground of Management and Editorial in the long decades of The Wall.

Mumbai's executive men's toilet has survived all the makeovers of the august 3rd floor management hall to which it has always been attached. It is historic in its own way because it was the only common ground of Management and Editorial in the long decades of The Wall.

It is tucked in discreetly near the hall's entrance. But not that discreetly. The senior editorial staff would walk across the no-man's-land of the lift landing and infiltrate into the 'enemy' side whenever needed. Some needed more often than others. One of Pradeep Guha's vivid memories of his rookie days in the advertising department is that of AS Abraham making "20 trips a day to the loo, and emerging buttoning his fly, continuing the procedure till he reached his own domain. The men would snigger, the women blush, but no one could summon the courage to buttonhole 'Abe'."

Remember, this was still the period of Editorial Supremacy, and any management guy daring to accost a lofty assistant editor would risk being struck down by lightning. In fact, if anyone from Advertising needed to talk to Editorial, he or she would have to enlist the services of the boss Thirumalai himself. He or his deputy, Prabir Roy. Being the son of the former GM, PK Roy, he had an inherited if uncodified clout.

LOO-NATIC ASYLUM

For the record, there is no executive women's toilet in either of the twin centres of Mumbai and Delhi. Nor is it needed. Interpret that as you will.

The economics whiz Swaminathan Anklesaria Aiyar had many quirks. As a genius he was entitled to the full quota. One of these was unique: he always carried his cup of tea to the 3rd floor loo in Times House, Delhi.

Mumbai's premium on space could never allow such a luxury, but in the earlier floor plan of the Delhi newsroom, the editor's cabin came with its own private toilet. The divinity could not be expected to tinkle with the hoi-polloi. This continued till Padgaonkar's time. Now, in the new democratisation, it's one for all, and all in one.

The rigours of coming to work on Mumbai's crowded trains, especially during the monsoon, when slush has to be negotiated along with the surge of dripping humanity, force the women to head for their toilet, and proceed to scrub their faces and arms at the wash basins. Sometimes near-baths are resorted to. No one uses the shower which has been considerately installed. But in addition to the instructions not to throw all the usually thrown into the toilets, there are such gems of printed notices as 'DO NOT WASH LEGS IN CUBICLES'.

The economics whiz Swaminathan Anklesaria Aiyar had many quirks. As a genius he was entitled to the full quota. One of these was unique: he always carried his cup of tea to the 3rd floor loo in Times House, Delhi.

At Khushwant Singh's *Illustrated Weekly of India* on the 4th floor of this building, sat R Gopalkrishna. The twice-born RGK was twice burdened by his karma here. On one side was the garrulous chief sub Jal Engineer, plaguing him with the most inane queries in long-drawn-out syllables ('Go-pal, where is Bho-pal?'); on the other side was the entrance to the toilets. What offended this elevated Brahmin even more than his neighbour's bugging was the fact that visitors would walk up to him and ask "Where's the loo?" The Brahmin would bristle: "How can they ask me this? And what is this word, 'loo'?

LOO-NATIC ASYLUM

Once in desperation he propped up a piece of cardboard on his desk on which he had written in capital letters, 'THIS MAN IS A DEAF MUTE'. But even this did not work. The outsiders kept coming up to his table with the offending query. He would silently point to the notice while looking straight ahead, puffing on his Charminar, and they would continue, "Yes, yes, but where is the loo?"

Perhaps they were as desperate as he was.

HRD TIMES

Jug Suraiya

Sorry, but this week I'm going to have to skip writing this column. The reason I'm having to give my column a miss this week is because of HRD. No, not Arjun Singh's HRD which has got people protesting on the streets all over and getting beaten up by the cops for their pains. The HRD that's dissuaded me from writing my column is my very own HRD, or rather TOI's very own HRD. And the instrument of HRD's dissuasion has come in the form of a voluminous sheaf of papers which in bulk and heft bears striking resemblance to an official report which might well be called Mandal Redux, or Son of Mandal Commission. In triplicate.

By way of introducing itself it says: 'Annual Assessment and Development Review (ADR) 2005-2006'. The 'twin objectives' of which are 'to evaluate employee performance for the stated period to arrive at key reward decisions. The Performance Assessment Template (Annexure 1) is to be used for recording the outcomes, as per process flow explained in Performance Assessment

HRD..
FORM A – Z
Desh ka Neta
like that only

Guidelines (Annexure 2)' and 'to evaluate employee potential and recommended training and development actions and draw up individual development plans. Employment Development Template (Annexure 3) is to be used for recording the outcomes, as per process flow explained in Employee Development Guideline (Annexure 4)'. This is on Page 1. After Page 1, there are 46 more pages. One of which, Page 5, says 'Preparing Job-function wise Employee Development Template based on Key Behaviours Dictionary (Annexure 7) and Key Behaviours Map (for HR use only) and communicating to Employees' who would 'require adhering to the following bell curve for linkage to individual reward and recognition decisions'.

Gripping stuff, if a bit cryptic. I'm tempted to do a Kaavya and bash out a Dan Brown rip-off called 'Da HRD Code'. But if I were to do that, who'd fill in my Performance Assessment Template (Annexure 1) to be used for recording the outcomes? Leave alone doing a Kaavya Dan Brown, I can't even take time off to do a Suraiya Jugular Vein. I can sense HRD peering over my shoulder, harrumphing impatience at my not getting on with following my bell curve for linkage as per process flow of Key Behaviours. I begin to feel a throbbing in my Templates, and suspect an acute onset of an Annexure-generated headache. The trouble is, I can either do my thing, which is writing this column, or I can evaluate employee potential and recommend training and development actions with respect to defined Key Result Areas, Measures & Standards. It's a no-contest. HRD outguns JV any day, and twice on Sundays. JV: 0; HRD: 1.

And I'm not alone. I can imagine Manmohanji, sitting there, head in his hands, wondering how to put the reservations genie back in the bottle and what to do about free trade agreements with ASEAN, when his HRD plonks an Annual Assessment and Development Review in front of him and tells him to get cracking, and mind you don't skip any Annexures, not to mention bell curves. So

Manmohanji puts aside the Indo-US strategic partnership, and FDI in retail and begins to fill in Template 1, as per HRD 's instructions. Except in his case, HRD is spelt with an 'S', for Soniaji. Or there's the other poor guy, trying to get his bow strung, when HRD in the form of Krishna hands him a potha of self-appraisal forms to fill in first, and Arjun's still looking up his Key Behaviours Map to see where 'Kurukshetra' is when the Kauravs launch a pre-emptive strike and cream the Pandavs and Vyas has to go back to the drawing board and rescript the Mahabharata, retitled MahaHRD.

Anyway, I'm finally done with my HRD paperwork, all 47 kg of it. And now I know why HRD is called HRD. It stands for Hernia Risk Development. In other words, a load of balls.

From The Times of India, May 21, 2006

IV

birth of a salesman

"It is difficult to separate, at times, the myth from the truth."

– Bob Kane –

"How will you negotiate
the choppy seas of Advertising
if you can't handle
those in a sheltered bay?"

VS TERROR-MALAI

VS Thirumalai ('Thiru'), tall, loose-limbed, dandily dressed and with a scones-meets-idlis accent succeeded MS Ahluwalia as head of the Advertising department after the latter's early death in the late 1960s. That unfortunate event had caused shock but no surprise since cirrhosis was the natural companion of a man who was not to be found in his office after 12.30 pm, and all business meetings after that time had to be held in the convivial Sardar's favourite bar near Flora Fountain. Agency bosses sighed in grief – and some relief.

Thiru's taste veered towards wine, and his drinking was merely one more aspect of his gentlemanly pursuits. Like his late afternoon spins around the Apollo Bunder harbour in a billowing Seabird.

Those whom he initiated into the mystique of the mille rate were taken out to sea, and then Thiru would say in a voice definitely calmer than the waters, "Okay old chaps, you are now on your own." If you turned green around the gills, he'd smirk, "How will you negotiate the choppy seas of Advertising if you can't handle those in a sheltered bay?" The newbie Chinnen Das was scared skiff of being singled out for such attention. He was convinced that he was going to meet a watery and premature end.

Thiru also introduced the matrimonial columns and the Appointments page to the TOI. And the idea of lemon tea.

For all his social gregariousness, Thirumalai struck terror in his staff. Everyone was petrified of his call. The red buzzer button outside his door would go on, and his peon would go in. Like most of his ilk, Ramchandran knew his proxy power well. He would emerge from his boss's room and walk, in sadistically slow motion, towards the row of desks where the ad executives sat quaking and hoping that the bell didn't toll for them. He would stop at the marked man, and announce in funereal tones, 'Saab bolaya'.

Thiru also introduced the matrimonial columns and the Appointments page to the TOI.
And the idea of lemon tea.

In fact one of their number, Nagrath, was so traumatised that he always had to make a loo stop before entering the dragon's lair.

Among the first and most successful women whom Thiru brought aboard his advertising ship was Fawzia Madni, in 1980. Here is her description of the Thiru summons. "Pradeep and Chinnen were then in their 20s and the department's cool dudes, their shirts open almost to their waists. They were usually the chosen quarry.

"As soon as Ramchandran approached, PG would hastily button his shirt right up to his collar. Chinnen would roll down his sleeves and button up the cuffs. In the monsoon months, he would also have to quickly struggle into his damp shoes and socks. Then the prey would walk trembling into the lion's den, saying their last prayers."

VS TERROR-MALAI

What was the usual cause of Thiru's fury? Simply, 'Why was this ad not in our paper?' 'Why are you not meeting more clients?' His way of checking (spying) on his staff was to phone advertising agencies and ask chattily, 'So which of my colleagues have you been meeting lately?'

Thiru's first hollering was the baptism of fire. Newbies would wait in trepidation for this anointing. Once three of the women ad officers decided to bunk, and go shoe-shopping to the Oberoi. There was an irresistible sale. As luck would have it, at the Flora Fountain traffic signal, Thiru's Ambassador drew up alongside their cab. All three instinctively ducked to the floor, and a trembling Fawzia refused to get up even "after his car had just passed us by without a gun being thrust out and fired at us. We could have been officially sharing a taxi for calls to Nariman Point, but Thiru had this terrifying hold over us."

Pradeep Guha described Thirumalai as 'a maverick but inspirational boss', and added with the superciliousness of the successor who took the job into a new paradigm, "He wouldn't have survived in today's market. He was essentially a monopolist, trigger-happy, shooting at agencies with disdain." But PG conceded, "Thiru taught me corporate arrogance. He told me, 'Unless you behave like a monopoly, no one will treat you like a monopoly'."

Pradeep Guha described Thirumalai as 'a maverick but inspirational boss'.

Scion of an old Iyengar family, VS Thirumalai was deeply religious and traditional. He visited Tirupati regularly, and it was in Chennai on a trip back from the pilgrimage that he died of a massive stroke in 1982. The next day, there was a mysterious fire only in his office in the TOI building at Bori Bunder. None of the adjacent cabins had so much as a singe, but every single one of Thiru's books, papers and personal files was burnt to cinders. "We all saw it for ourselves, it happened around noon."

GHOST WRITING

When the Business Director, T Pithavala died, watchmen whispered that after they had shut down the power for the night, lights would suddenly spring to life only in his office room. "Han saab, sirf unkey kamrey mein."

Thirumalai's is just one of the spooky stories from the 107-year-old Times of India building since, like every self-respecting castle, hoary corporate palaces too must have their resident ghosts. When the Business Director, T Pithavala died, watchmen whispered that after they had shut down the power for the night, lights would suddenly spring to life only in his office room. "Haan saab, sirf unkey kamrey mein."

There were other ghosts too which were laid by the spanky new makeover – some might say frightened away by Hafeez Contractor's signature flamboyance. But enough dark nooks and crannies have escaped a succession of interior designers to allow for things that go bump on an extraordinarily harried – or imaginative – night.

At least two of them were summoned in a planchette as a group of Response executives sat desperately trying to stave off sleep and boredom. A huge and prolonged downpour had flooded out all transportation, so they had to spend the night in the office. This was several years before the Deluge of 26/7/2005.

A colonial hangover, literally, was the ghost of a hated Englishman who prowled about the fourth floor of the building, and was in fact the figment of convenience of those who used to stay behind to drink in the after-hours darkness. After his stint as Branch head in the Ahmedabad office, Arun Arora came to Mumbai at the end of 1981 in charge of the newly created Development (later upgraded to Modernisation). The management didn't seem to have much hope for it because he was given a tiny windowless cubicle on this floor. In fact, it was part of a larger cabin, and comprised only an editorial table cut into two, with an opaque-glass screen around it. The magazine edit teams would all leave by 5.50 pm, and by 6.30 or so, the door of the main cabin was locked.

One night, Arora got locked in. There was no night operator so he could not phone for help. He kept thinking of the ghost. So, unfortunately did the watchmen, because when he began banging on his door to draw attention, it only resulted in them fleeing in panic. In vain did he shout, 'Come back, come back. I'm Arun Arora.' He was only rescued at 10 pm by a durwan braver than his colleagues.

One night, Arora got locked in. There was no night operator so he could not phone for help. He kept thinking of the ghost. So, unfortunately did the watchmen, because when he began banging on his door to draw attention, it only resulted in them fleeing in panic.

'BOSS'

Samir Jain's stamp began to be seen all over the company in the mid-1980s. He decreed that it should be run not as a newspaper house, but as a business house.

Journalists in course of time came around to writing for the reader rather than for their sources, their Press Club audience, and their own glory. On occasions, they slipped up and said 'product' instead of 'paper'. But what took the longest to accept was the new corporate wisdom that a newspaper was not some exalted entity, but simply a service industry, and must be marketed in much the same way. It demolished the much-vaunted mystique of the profession, indeed the near divine right of editors.

The end customer became not the reader, but the advertiser. The Circulation (rechristened Research and Market Development, RMD) department's target was not a diwan-e-aam, but a diwan-e-khaas of readership – the right kind of readers who would attract the right kind of advertising. The analogy of airlines was used: They make their profits from the select top end of the plane, not from the masses packed into Coach class. Naturally, it followed that the Advertising (rechristened Response) department became the strategic battalion, and Pradeep Guha its starred General.

Pradeep Guha (later just 'Boss' when addressed by his team) had joined the TOI as a

Marxist-turned-advertising executive in 1973. His starting salary was Rs 750. He went on to become one of the most powerful men in Bennett, and by that token, all media.

He left after 30 years to join another media house. But he still retains his appointment letter. This is the hold of the TOI, and many similar, yellowing letterheads are lovlying preserved in the files and drawers of other old-Times-ers.

His first recollection from a memorable innings was the line that snaked all the way outside the building, waiting to enter the Classifieds section which was on the ground floor. The queue was always there, in humid heat or ruthless Mumbai monsoon. Today, this department is on a better-segmented and swanky mezzanine, with soothing potted plants and a comfortable waiting lounge.

But he [Pradeep Guha] still retains his appointment letter. This is the hold of the TOI.

In his grade at that time, the annual increment was Rs 25. One year, "I got six, and even though that toted up to the grand figure of just Rs150, there was a palpable animosity among my colleagues." It gave the one-time communist student leader his "first glimpse of the dog-eats-dog corporate life".

Maybe you hated him for his highhandedness, but you had to admire Pradeep Guha for his creative genius. The VC's unquestioning support, allowed him to cut a swathe across the TOI's blinkered bureaucracy and established norms. This special position explained a great deal of his success.

Guha was not a babu or a bean counter. He was an entrepreneur and a doer, a double-defiance of the Bengali stereotype of the languorous intellectual with a disdain for lowbrow lucre. Meetings summoned by him were one-sided affairs. They would begin by people putting out their great ideas, while Boss sat immersed in his own thoughts, chewing his fingers down to their nail-beds. Then, taking no cognisance at all of anything that had had been said, he would launch into a monologue laying out fully and precisely what had to be done. No one interjected.

'BOSS'

If it sounds like the word of God, that's exactly how his Response team at least perceived it. They worshipped him, and he loved the adulation, even sycophancy. But his team also genuinely liked him because he seldom subjected them to the abrasiveness arrogance with which he treated agencies and advertisers. Editorial heads also deferred to him, even if they differed. His writ would run anyway. To be honest, it would work out brilliantly. And, to be fair, he would take responsibility for it if it didn't.

If the Bangalore edition achieved the incredible turnaround it did in so short a span, it was because he was the facilitating director. He sanctioned the technological equipment needed to achieve the sleek look with a speed unknown in the TOI. And, thuck-thuck-thuck, in the course of 15 minutes one morning, he sorted out the pagination which the senior editors had struggled with for days.

The Femina-Miss India contest used to be a jumped-up college pageant, a guarantor of a rich and famous husband, a social hand-out to clients and friends, or simply an ego massage for the editor and the GM. Yes the dusky, leggy medical student, Reita Faria, had been crowned Miss World in 1965, but that was a flash in the pancake makeup. Pradeep Guha turned it from a home production into a global blockbuster. From a contest to a brand.

He did it with the driven single-mindedness with which the former Soviet countries had turned out Olympics gold medallists or Richard Williams turned Venus and Serena into winning machines. The intensive grooming process became an industry or several, from dress to deportment

Guha was not a babu or a bean counter.
He was an entrepreneur and a doer,
a double-defiance of the Bengali stereotype
of the languorous intellectual
with a disdain for lowbrow lucre.

to dance to the deft handling of every possible question that could be thrown at the hapless girl in the heat of the arc lights. Poise under pressure was drilled into her with the dedication of a Mastermind contest or a military academy.

'BOSS'

Yes, girls were groomed for the earlier contests, but it was with limited resources and goals. Pradeep Guha, the ringmaster, put it this way: "They were looking at creating a Miss India. I was looking at creating a Miss World and a Miss Universe incidentally from India." Aishwarya Rai and Sushmita Sen began an epidemic of titles. India's eyes and mouth formed the same 'O' of disbelief as that first photograph of Sushmita winning the Miss Universe title at Manila in 1994.

These global wins spawned fashion, beauty and grooming industries even in small towns. Feminists may scowl, but it was decidedly a stiletto strut into empowerment.

When PG left the organisation after almost 30 years, a human chain from the 2nd floor to the gate lined up tearfully to bid him farewell.

We will meet Guha again with and in 'The Triumvirate,'

***

And here's a story to show that the money-machine could be anything but….

Two years into Pradeep Guha's powerful stewardship of Response, and his raking in the moolah by the shovelful for the group, the Chairman Ashok Jain turned to his son, Samir just after PG left the room, and ingenuously asked, "Achcha, yeh banda karta kya hai?" (What exactly does this chap do in the organisation?)

Clearly, Ashok Jain belonged to a less profit-centric time.

It called for an entire mindset change.

MASTER MOVE

The VC's genius for striking gold was on display in the shift from the column centimetre to the square centimetre as the measure for the rate for display ads. It called for an entire mindset change, but the internal pessimism and external resistance crumbled under the force of his persistence. In course of time, the rate even crossed the psychological five-digit barrier.

The VC ingeniously split the col cm into sq cms, charging, in the premium editions, Rs 3,000 per the latter instead of Rs 9,000 for the former. On the surface, it looked like a cut, but was in fact a jump. The col cm now totalled Rs 12,000. In the many-layered space-buying process, this sleight of hand escaped notice till the practice was underway. Within a month, four of the other major national newspaper groups had also shifted to the sq cm.

The VC's Mastermind was just that. With it, the advertiser paid just one rupee per col cm in TOIBg. The trick, of course, was that he had to club together other editions to avail of this sweetener.

The dress code was 'black tie'.
Having no clue of what this meant,
and going by the obvious,
the three rushed out and bought just that.

BLACKENED TIE

As the promising young men of what was still the Advertising department, Chinnen Das, Bhaskar Das and R Sundar were invited by PG to what was just becoming the new social affectation, the 'wine and cheese' party. The dress code was 'black tie'. Having no clue of what this meant, and going by the obvious, the three rushed out and bought just that. They were the only ones that evening in long black ties – and long red faces.

BHASKARISMS

Pradeep Guha's successor as head of Response is a character more in the mould of Guha's predecessor, Thirumalai. Bhaskar Das has got over his penchant for red-streaked locks layered in edgy haircuts. He strikes no terror in his staff, but he can knock you down in a tsunami of Bhaskarisms, a tidal wave of inimitable, unstoppable words and expressions. When you recover your senses, you will find that it isn't gobbledy-gook 'jaar-gon'; it is actually his equally unorthodox prescription for management wellness.

Let Dr Das speak for himself. Incidentally he rattled this off in the course of 30 minutes while waiting to take a fog-delayed flight. The jury is still out on whether this worsened, if not actually caused, the airport's problem

On the specialness of TOI

When one spends a whole career in one single company, it becomes "special" by default. Can you imagine how may times this 178-year-old company has been reinvented? And that too by grey-haired revolutionaries like me. Moreover, this re-invention is not just the once-in-a decade kind. Operating in a hyper-competitive and dynamic environment that experiences nano-second revision in market realities, the key skill-set has been the organisation's ability to re-invent 'on the go'.

Lehman Brothers became a victim of a disruptive economy after 171 years as they could not perhaps read the writing on the wall. But, in our case, our incumbency was never a burden. In fact, it has constantly energised us to be an insurgent simultaneously. It might be oxymoronish to even think about an insurgent spirit within an incumbent body. That is possible in a company that nurtures and encourages intelligent naivety wherein the incumbency helps focus on the course of success but simultaneously also nurtures an intelligent innocence about the future. As a result, it is not merely a humdrum business of commerce. It's about continuously engaging organizational conscience in a 'future-backward' strategy and not simply a 'present-forward' approach (that afflicts most organisations). So, companies need to jettison bias for 'nostalgia' (positive memories of past performance) for 'postalgia' (desired positive memory of future) instead.

BHASKARISMS

Success has a built-in learning disability. This organisation has to fight this infection by destroying a number of business models at the height of its success. When you have a new product, every day, for 362 days a year, decoding the tectonic shift in the reader's taste-space is more an art than a science. To that extent the organisational DNA has to constantly evolve an advance version of business thoughtware. There is no fool-proof formula for that. It co-evolves with our stakeholders through a socio-digital cultural process of evolution.

In this company one gets value addition by osmosis from all the internal stakeholders; in the case of VC, we should call that 'cosmosis'. Even after 30 years, I am a perpetual learner (Bhaskar got his Ph.D after working in the company for 29 years) and, as such, it has a huge impetus for growing in the company.

He strikes no terror
in his staff,
but he can knock you down
in a tsunami of Bhaskarisms,
a tidal wave of inimitable,
unstoppable words
and expressions.

On its mythology

A brand becomes a myth when it migrates from the explicit to the implicit, from the tangible to the visceral, from the mundane to the psychic level. So, for me, or for that matter for any brand-vocate of any newspaper brand, TOI is a way of life and a celebration of existence as opposed to the general perception of a newspaper company being a purveyor of news. A mythology is supposed to energize and sanitize internal cultural processes of an organisation. It uplifts a pedestrian activity into a sublime one. TOI mythology has been happening in a sustained manner based on tacit understanding about any mind product: 'in any mind product the subliminal aspiration of users will always be at variance with their articulated intent.' This superordinate philosophy lifts the entire content aggregation to the realm of architecture and craftsmanship. And with TOI doing it for 178 years, perhaps it has become part of its own genetic code.

On making a happy newspaper

Happiness is an outcome. Hence, it cannot be a part of any objective. Moreover, happiness of human beings is an inside-out process and not an outside-in process. Consequently, every individual is alike in happiness but, are different in unhappiness. A happy newspaper is something that makes the reader see the positive sides of life – whether it is positive escapism or positive awareness.

Come to think of it, every media facilitates escapism, and escapism is a great free of cost tourist spot. Escapism is not negative. It helps make a positive outcome of a negative situation. People are fully aware of their respective challenges of life. They don't need reinforcement of those realities through an intermediary. What they need is a facilitation to develop copabilities to

THE HAPPY TIMES OF INDIA

overcome the challenges of life. They need to be upgraded so that they remain successful and get entertained through the complete value chain of life. In other words, happy papers are trusted family members that help one navigate the continuously fluid challenges of life.

On selling space

In a media space that is continuously getting morphed into new realities due to ubiquitous and accelerated pace of technology change, focusing on selling space or on the supply side of the business is prehistoric and myopic. It is important to focus on the demand side (upstream marketing) instead of mere supply side (downstream marketing) of space selling. In fact, contextually, relevant content creation for the demand side is a pre-condition of any successful business model.

The word consumer/reader presupposes that someone is consuming or reading a paper. In a new socio-digital world, this axiom would not be accepted. The new axiom of content creation is that it must make people engage continuously and immerse in an experience that is memorable and valuable to their life. This is the key part of business now, because content creation is in a permanent beta state and one is only as good as the last content creation. The more relevant the content is in the user's life, the better is the traction for the reader. When that happens all marketing communicators participate in creating contextualised communication that facilitates reader search for solution.

On winning awards

Any award has a narcotic value as it creates an enlarged image of oneself. But ideally an award should propel an individual/organization to achieve higher levels of perfection. It must create individual humility and help internalize the responsibility that the awarder has conferred on them to remain as a lighthouse beacon of standards. In an era of five minutes of fame, huge commoditization has also taken place in the space of awards. Hence, it is imperative to 'brand the experience', as opposed to execute an award programme to expand the experience of the brand. The referral value of an award is ultimately a testimony to the trust that the brand represents for the consumers. This is also unique because while other brands talk about this we talk about our reader's domain of interest and amplify that.

In the case of TOI, awards have not been able to distract us from the core objective that our brands have been engaged in for so many years – i.e. 'upgrading readers in their pursuits of life'. In that task, we have gone beyond reportage and have taken up national issues of governance, leadership, mass movement of literacy and even global issues like regional collaboration for peace and prosperity. This is also unique because, while other brands talk about themselves as newspapers, we talk about reader's domain of interest.

One more perspective…

Future of journalism

Future is not what happens to an organization – future is what the organization creates for itself. So, it is more a crafting process then a `happenstance' process. I think news and journalism (that facilitates enlightenment and upgradation of perspectives) will always remain relevant and critical for navigation of life. But in the new digital world, users will be platform agnostic and content creators and organizations have to be skilled in embracing digital and analog culture simultaneously.

The divide of on-live and off-live will be blurred in favour of 'through the live'. So while one-to-million news of information dissemination will continue, one-to-one interaction, expression of opinion and community discussion, sharing of information (thanks to Facebook, Twitter and micro blogs) will happen simultaneously. So, format neutrality and adoption of broadcatching mentality (as opposed to broadcasting i.e. radiating the same content across multiple formats of distribution and access by a consumer) will be the survival mantra. Organizations need to lose control to retain control across spectrums of stakeholders and mine crowd intelligence for developing a synthesized version of content that is collaborative and trustworthy. The adoption of this principle can make the future less tense.

BHASKARISMS

It emphasized the pre-eminent position of this wealth-creating department [Response],and as much that of its whiz-head, Pradeep Guha.

THE GAIN IN SPAIN

International Response conferences became the talk of the organisation. Starting in 1993, this was the first time that a large team was being taken abroad at company expense, and it was a huge leap in corporate culture. It emphasised the pre-eminent position of this wealth-creating department, and as much that of its whiz-head, Pradeep Guha. It also reflected the increasing international presence in the Times Group, and its own globalization. The exposure was part of the company's investment in the personal and professional growth of its talent pool.

The first outing was to Nepal. But the big ones were in Kenya, the Europe trip with London, Paris, Brussels and Amsterdam, Sun City-Johannesburg, Egypt-Cyprus-Jerusalem, and in 2008, Turkey.

Samir Jain was keen on taking the team to Las Vegas to show its unique business model. The drinks are priced low so that the slot machines and the gaming tables rake in more – but it didn't happen. These conferences were bonding exercises, the glue coming from travelling and doing fun things as a group and also from joking together, and about each other.

THE GAIN IN SPAIN

There was the joke about the three Pradeeps. Pradeep Khaitan was the 'boardroom voice'; Pradeep Guha was the 'bedroom voice' and the third Pradeep, who shall be mercifully left unidentified, was the 'boredom voice'.

Expectedly, it was Pradeep Guha, soon the 'Boss' of Response, who was the major domo of the conferences. But he was not just the head; he was also the heart. In Australia, they had gone scuba diving. Pradeep waited on shore till each one had gone down – and come up. Which was when it was pointed out that the 'PG' of his initials was the same as the code on movies: Parental Guidance. He was always there for the team. In Jerusalem, someone's wallet was lost, and PG paid all his expenses from his own pocket.

He [Pradeep Guha] was always there for the team.

The Response conference in Spain was special in many ways. Samir Jain and Meera Jain came along, as they did for several others. The meal allowance was $10 per day, and realising that it wouldn't go far to achieve the desired exposure to fine living, the VC constantly footed the bill personally. He took great interest in fine food as an idea and a trend, though he was strictly vegetarian, ate sparely, and of course never touched anything remotely alcoholic.

The women of Response, Indira Deish, Teena Singh, Fawzia Madni and Niloufer Bilimoria, gave full play to his desire to indulge his team. One evening, they spied him in a very tempting ice-cream parlour. So they all sauntered in, knowing full well that that he would pay. He did, and egged them on to try out as many exotic sundaes as their gluttony desired.

They all trooped off to see a bullfight in Madrid. And when the master of ceremonies asked for a volunteer from the crowd, a Response executive, Adil Warsi, jumped in, and did the few flourishes with the matador's cloak that he was asked to do – just as a performance. VC got so excited that he presented Warsi not the traditional 'both ears and the tail of the vanquished bull', but something more in keeping with his pacifist Jain philosophy, and more useful too: $200.

*For Pradeep Guha,
Mrs Jain chose something unique:
it was from a store called 'PG',
so the carrier bag became
more coveted
than the expensive contents.*

Indira was more thrilled by her trophy: a kiss planted on her cheek by VC. Alas, proof was not captured for posterity. So her colleague Debashish Ghosh was summoned with his camera, and the VC gamely gave an encore.

On the last day, there was a surprise announcement. Everyone got $200 to go buy any electronic item they wanted from Duty Free, but it had to be business related, a tape recorder, a camera or the like. Indira got her first fancy perfume too, on this trip, a Goya, a gift from Meera Jain. For Pradeep Guha, Mrs Jain chose something unique: it was from a store called 'PG', so the carrier bag became more coveted than the expensive contents.

Before they went international, Response conferences were held at different Indian destinations. The first one was Surajkund, outside Delhi, in 1984. The second was in Agra, and it was memorable for reasons other than the Taj. Samir Jain, then designated Joint MD, spoke about the Big 'O' – that was what a placement in the TOI should give the advertiser. The conventional marketing mantra of 'customer delight' had just been sexed up. It scandalised the seniors, but it became unmistakably clear that the regime change would put an end to business as it had been known in the past 147 years.

Teena and Indira also remember the Agra conference because they were newbies, and PG, then still a senior manager, gave the two of them a motivational award. They got it for the best presentation, and also for asking the most questions.

THE GAIN IN SPAIN

At Agra, everyone was young and carefree. At a dinner party, Nandita Jain asked Indira to get Samir Jain on the floor. He gamely agreed, and "to the surprise of all, danced fabulously." Indira added, "He then defied me to get Baljit Kapoor on the floor too. That old bulldog of 60, he too agreed. Apparently, Samir had made an offer of Rs 1,000 to anyone who could make Mr Kapoor dance. Everyone was too scared to approach him. But I was young and brash, and asked him in my bindaas Punjabi kudi fashion. I got a 'special award' for my gutsiness."

LATE LATIFA

"PG offered to get me alarm clocks
of ascending decibels,
and once said, only half in jest,
'OK, come home with me
after work every night,
and I will bring you to office
the next day on time in my car'!"

In the Response department, Niloufer and Fawzia had their own rivalries less public than those of editorial's 'petticoat wars', but they were bound inseparably by their habitual and incurable late-coming. Niloufer laughed about it." PG offered to get me alarm clocks of ascending decibels, and once said, only half in jest, 'OK, come home with me after work every night, and I will bring you to office the next day on time in my car'!'"

At the Response Conferences at exotic destinations, Niloufer and Fawzia were always the last to come, huffing and puffing and apologising, to the meeting or to be back on the bus during the sightseeing and (more so) shopping trips.

At the one in Spain, everyone was supposed to assemble in the hotel lobby at 4 am to take the coach to the airport. Tired of being branded Late Latifa, Fawzia landed up there at 3.30 am, and waited patiently in the empty expanse, feeling groggy but mighty pleased at her feat. Instead of praising her for finally being not just on time, but actually half an hour early, Pradeep dismissively said, "What do you mean you deserve a pat on the back? It just proves that timing means nothing to you. Either you are too early or you are too late."

LATE LATIFA

Realizing that there was no wining in this game, Fawzia skulked away to catch the bus, consoling herself that at least she hadn't missed it.

AD AND MINUS

Ads are as much the targets of law suits as articles and reports.

Ads are as much the targets of law suits as articles and reports. Remember the long-drawn out obscenity case against the Madhu Sapre-Milind Soman Tuff Shoes-Python ad? Editors may have left, the publication may have shut down, even the targeted company may have gone out of business, but like the karmic cycle, there is no getting off. The case continues its relentless journey through the courts. This happened with the Mexx ad and The Metropolis on Saturday in which it had been published. The former editor, former publisher and the advertising agency still had to make their appearances before the judge – with the plaintiff himself choosing to stay away.

NON-STIMULUS OF RESPONSE

But the grand money-machine of Response sometimes develops cogs that squeak for lack of oiling, read, 'encouragement'.

It has been run by highly admired, almost-worshipped Supremos, but the grand money- machine of Response sometimes develops cogs that squeak for lack of oiling, read, 'encouragement'.

In the realm of management by initials, meetings are referred to this way as well as bosses. Among the former were the MRMs – Monthly Review Meetings – attended by 10 heads from different Response centres. After the rounds of Cochin, Hyderabad, Kolkata, some of them suggested the more exotic locale of Leh. Unfortunately it was scuttled by a consortium. Bhaskar Das said the rarefied air of Ladakh would need acclimatisation, and he coopted the non-Bong Das, Chinnen, to support this objection. They took it to Pradeep Guha who, in a show of chauvinistic solidarity, took their side.

As it happened, this Femina initiative turned a languishing 'C' market into an 'A' market.

Another MRM was to be held in Sri Lanka. Niloufer Bilimoria, then handling International, thought it would be a great idea to stay one more day and check out the market. She set up meetings in advance hoping to launch an ad-led Femina edition there. She excitedly clicked off in her trade-mark stiletto sandals to PG, who promptly said, "Rubbish! What business are you going to get in that war-torn country?" She kept badgering him till he finally gave in, saying, "Do what you want as long as you don't involve me, and you don't take the company to the cleaners."

As it happened, this *Femina* initiative turned a languishing 'C' market into an 'A' market. The rates were low, but there was real advertising potential. The successful magazine coming here sent out a strong signal of confidence, which broke the ravaged island's jinx of 'Don't go there. You'll lose your job or your life'.

Then there was G Krishnan, not very popular in certain quarters, not least because he chose to hold his meetings till late. "We would be starving, and would pointedly eat biscuits, but he refused to take the hint."

Fawzia had worked on a presentation for PG till 2 am, and arrived bleary-eyed the next morning. Boss, assuming that this was once again her late-Latifa problem, sarcastically said, "Did you wake up in time even to brush your teeth?" A sleep-deprived Fawzia shot back, "If I stand here long enough you'll find out." She then added for good measure, "This nasty streak of yours, does it come naturally? Or do you practise it every morning in front of your shaving mirror?"

But in these furnaces, close bonds were tempered. Behind PG's gruffness was genuine caring for his team, and his brilliance blinded out all his sins. Sooner or later.

V

view from the top

"Myths, whether in written or visual form, serve a vital role of asking unanswerable questions and providing unquestionable answers."

– Michael Shermer –

ONCE UPON A TRIUMVIRATE

Somehow survived the 'matrix style'...

Pradeep Guha may have given the impression that he called all the shots, but there were other generals too.

For almost 15 years, just below the Jains sat a powerful triumvirate comprising, in alphabetical order, Arun Arora, Pradeep Guha and Vijay Jindal. They held sway over clearly defined and jealously guarded territories which had somehow survived the 'matrix style' that Samir Jain introduced in the 1990s. The shift from a silo/function-driven company to one with cross-functional linkages, synergy and a holistic world-view would begin to happen only when the millennium itself changed.

You might care to draw an analogy with the Tata Group. This too had operated through fiefdoms during JRD's regime, and here too the feudal satraps had to leave before the Ratan-ordained changeover could be complete.

Ravi Dhariwal, who joined from Pepsico, quickly made his assessments with an 'outsider's' insight. The small-built 'PG' was a tall leader, and treated like royalty; he was brilliant, but he put his Response department first, and the company second. Jindal was the contrarian thinker; you went to him for advice when you needed an out-of-the-box perspective. He was an expert at using the law and its loopholes to serve a corporate purpose. He never felt the need to persuade, people acceded simply because he said so. The hard-core rivalry was between Guha and Jindal. Arora was the tech guy, and they left him pretty much alone because it was somewhat out of their interest.

Ravi added, “PG was VC’s comrade-in-arms; he really loved him. Jindal was his sparring partner. And Arora was his executive arm who also cut out the noise that VC never wanted to hear.” He has blandly stated on several occasions that the king has to be cocooned from the outside world, and “Arun did that particularly well.”

The best stories about Vijay Jindal are all in Punjabi, and suffer irretrievably in translation. In any language however, the rivalry among the triumvirate remains undiminished. When Jindal joined Zee as its executive head, he crowed, ‘See where I am and see where Pradeep is.’ But Pradeep was to follow him there many years later. He did not retort, ‘See, here I am.’

Vijay Jindal’s first steps towards the inner circle are as remarkable as his later trajectory. He was working as an assistant to Atma Ram Sarogi, an important functionary in S.P. Jain’s set up. One day Samir Jain had gone over to meet Sarogi, where Jindal happened to be having lunch. He merely made eye contact with him, but told Sarogi to send him to his office. After a perfunctory talk, VC put Jindal in charge of the finance companies of Bennett. Then he was made GM and CGM of Delhi branch, after which he rose to Director and finally Board Director.

This gizmo [multiple CD player overshadowed the car itself, and it was the first feature which he pointed out to everyone who came down to admire the acme of automobile technology.

A'S B AND ITS CD

Arun Arora got the company's first Mercedes Benz, but the man whose technology decisions had such an impact on the company's fortunes was most excited over the accessory of the multiple CD player. This gizmo overshadowed the car itself, and it was the first feature which he pointed out to everyone who came down to admire the acme of automobile technology. A colleague suspected that it was more to experience – and show off – the CD changer that Arun invited him for a drive to Mumbai's Haji Ali. They stopped there for a fruit cream at the famous Juice Centre, before purring back. The CD changer, alas, did not get much of a chance to do its number during the not-so-long spin.

SESQUI... WHAT?

"Make him say 'sesquicentennial'."

1988-1989 was the year of the sesquicentennial, as the 150-year jubilee was rather pretentiously referred to. One suspects no one would have heard of the word had it not been used by La Martiniere for its own celebrations a while earlier. It may or may not have been at the suggestion of its two bright young alumni who had a year or so ago come over to the TOI from The Statesman, Chandan Mitra and Swapan Dasgupta, neither of them yet saffronised.

It was another matter that most people mispronounced – and misspelt-the 'sesquicentennial'. It was such a tongue-twister that PG Wodehouse fans on the editorial floor joked that it could easily have replaced Bertie Wooster's formula for checking if a person was drunk: "Make him say 'British Constitution'." The new variation could be "Make him say 'sesquicentennial'."

Nomenclature apart, the sesquicentennial was a turning point. It turned the Old Lady of Bori Bunder into a power babe, yes, but, at its white-hot core, it changed the Times of India from a newspaper into a brand. This was Samir Jain's vision for his 150-year-old legacy, and the celebrations were the creation of his vivacious sister, Nandita. The base-line of the celebrations was 'Good Times, Sad Times, Changing Times'.

The men who helped give all this a tangible form were Pradeep Guha, the advertising boss, and Pritish Nandy who had come to Bennett at the end of 1982, as Group Editor & Publishing Director – and "put in charge of the *Illustrated Weekly Filmfare*, *The Independent*, *Evening News* – anything that no one else could run" as he described it with typical modesty. In the Gospel according to Nandy, "Journalists thought all this brand business was poppycock, if not actually heresy."

SESQUI…WHAT?

Pritish was assigned the task of orchestrating the events which would establish the brand. With trademark bluster, Nandy recalled, "I told Samir that I couldn't deal with the TOI bureaucracy. Everybody and his grandfather think that Pritish Nandy can do anything. But I can do eff-all if I have to encounter babu-giri at every stage." Nandita reassured him with her natural charm, "Nandy-ji don't worry – leave them to me." But when Nandita entered the picture, Pritish had asked Samir, "Do you want to police me through your sister?" "No, no,' he had replied, starting to laugh in his way which meant 'Partly yes.'

The idea was to do iconic stuff at the sesquicentennial. To dream big and do big. To show scale, size, imagination and power and in a way that could only be done by the Times of India. The jubilee was also seized as an opportunity for the paper to reconnect with the city of its birth. The jubilee kicked off on November 3, 1988 with Prime Minister Rajiv Gandhi coming to Mumbai to release a commemorative stamp with Laxman's common man on a gold background.

Mumbai was then the unchallenged centre of the art world, and Nandy's Weekly had been a big promoter of artists. So the Command Centre sat down to think, 'How do we create the biggest art event? Let's do it right in the throbbing heart of Bombay – VT station.' The immediate response was 'Are you MAD? It'll get vandalized by the aam janata. We'll have to spend a fortune on security!' Nandy replied, 'Trust me, we won't need security. I'll take responsibility for each and every work. In any case, we will insure the exhibition.'

The idea was to do iconic stuff at the sesquicentennial. To dream big and do big.

Timeless Art opened to disbelief and awe, the foyer of the station itself converted into a masterpiece with the lighting which played up the otherwise unnoticed architectural embellishments of Frederick William Steven's Bombay Gothic creation. For the next couple of weeks, the aam janta, far from vandalizing, were fascinated. The millions who travelled on the local trains had never been exposed to such an aesthetic; indeed had never seen in such a spectacular light the station they had hurried through all their lives. They stood and stared and appreciated – and let their homebound trains leave without them. Dinner could wait. When again would they be able to feast on such a spread?

The still relatively unknown Astad Deboo added his touch of desi-global to the inauguration. He was India's first exponent of modern dance, combining his training in Bharat Natyam, Kuchipudi and Kathak with the choreography mastered under the legendary Martha Graham. It was gamble choosing him to complement the opening of Timeless Art, but all doubts were dispersed as he snaked his way from VT station to the JJ school of Art, the well-heeled audience doing its own Guccipudi as it followed this sinuous and gaunt Pied Piper to the exhibition's opening party in these magically lit grounds amidst brooding ancient banyans.

It was decided to climax the exhibition with an auction. And of course it couldn't be some local auctioneer. A grandnephew of the Scots poet, Walter de la Mare, agreed to wield the hammer. It was the first spectacular art auction in India, 'with a gora thrown in for good effect,' as Nandy put it. Why, even in the annals of Sotheby's itself, it was acclaimed as an unprecedented auction of contemporary figurative work. It showcased the work of 35 individuals, representing a broad array of senior and junior artists. And it catapulted many into the international arena: Nalini Malani, Manjit Bawa, NS Bendre, Bhupen Khakhar, Manu Parekh, Madhvi Parekh, Gieve Patel, Alex Mathew, Tyeb Mehta, Mrinalini Mukherjee, Pushpamala N, DLN Reddy, Ravinder Reddy, Himmat Shaw, GM Sheikh, Nilima Sheikh, KG Subramanyan and Vivan Sundaram.

SESQUI...WHAT?

The venue again was unprecedented: the training ship 'Jawahar', a concrete leviathan in the high-security Navy Nagar. The auction was preceded by a champagne party so that wallets loosened up. Among the glitterati who trooped in was Bianca Jagger. The state Chief Minister Sharad Pawar got so carried away by the occasion that he announced that the government would donate a plot of land to the Bombay Art Society.

Among the successful bidders were the fabulously rich Hindujas. But they weren't the ones who made history that night. An MF Husain canvas drummed up the then unheard of figure of Rs 10 lakhs. Pritish's Weekly had done a cover story when one of his paintings crossed the Rs 1 lakh barrier. Husain went to a diamond merchant, and according to Nandy, "Rumour had it that the already controversial artist had struck a deal with the fellow: if he paid Rs 10 lakh at the auction, he'd give him three canvases on the side for free."

Husain went to a diamond merchant, and according to Nandy, "Rumour had it that the already controversial artist had struck a deal with the fellow: if he paid Rs 10 lakh at the auction, he'd give him three canvases on the side for free."

The other memorable sesquicentennial events were Unusual Ragas, all night and open air on the grounds of the Royal Western India Turf Club in Mumbai and Morning Ragas at Siri Fort in Delhi. This was done entirely by Nandita – ably supported by Neerja Shah, a bright young relative and friend of the Jains.

The sesquicentennial was also landmarked with the publication of eight lavish coffee table books, collating the best of the Times...

Like Samir and Nandita, she was part of the satsang of Mataji Laxmi, a Bandra-based guru.Many people believed that this 'satsang' was the sure route to these media barons. Years later, when Vivek Oberoi emerged on the screen, Suresh Oberoi tried getting closer to Samir at the satsang to push his son's case at Filmfare. Too bad, it didn't work that way with the Jains. In such matters, they kept state and church apart.

The sesquicentennial was also landmarked with the publication of eight lavish coffee table books, collating the best of the Times: Forefront, Viewpoint, Centrepiece, Feedback, The Eloquent Brush, Past Times, Flashback and Brand New. They are still treasured as collector's items. Less overwhelming were the four deconstructionist magazines on Culture, Society, Economy and Sport, produced by an imported American promptly called 'Connor-ji'. No one understood them.

Arguably, the biggest crowd-puller was the Human Rights Now concert held in Delhi's Jawaharlal Nehru stadium featuring Tracy Chapman, Peter Gabriel, Sting and Bruce Springstein. Mumbai got 'Europe' a rock concert, and Jazz featuring Charlie Byrd. Both cities got the YSL fashion show, both at never-before venues, the Gateway of India and Siri Fort.

The 'Changing Times' part of the sesquicentennial's slogan was most evident at the heritage building on Mumbai's DN Road. The entire interior was gouged and redesigned by the whiz architect, Hafeez Contractor (also snidely referred to as Full-fees Contractor).

The most flamboyant metamorphosis was that of the second floor. The once grimy, steamy typesetting room with its linotype machines was turned into a swish Response department (rechristened from the old Advertising department). It was the showpiece floor, most visited by outsiders, and it was replete with Rajasthani jharokas, framed copies of vintage ads and contemporary art. The old cast iron pillars with their decorative capitals were retained, but cheekily painted in brilliant blue and burnt orange.

SESQUI...WHAT?

The newsroom also got a makeover, but the Resident Editor, Darryl D'Monte, put his foot down over Hafeez's choice of flooring. If he hadn't, it would have slipped on the suggested granite. The newsroom was different from Response. Here, deadline-time hysteria did not allow the measured tread which the latter could indulge in, indeed cultivated. Bones would have been broken as reporters rushed about and the news editor grew ballistic. The rougher Kota stone was agreed upon.

"Where are the two old dummies?" And the redoubtable Unni replied, "They've gone for lunch."

OLD DUMMIES...

Darryl, along with several other old-Times-ers, had returned to the Bori Bunder building, persuaded back and happy to be part of the makeover of the Old Lady into a babe. He had been working on his own for the past eight years, had grown to be self-reliant, and was impatient when having to depend on others.

Darryl's irritation and nervous tic both got more pronounced when the TOI's sesquicentennial special issues had to be planned and produced. Several dummy layouts were made, discarded and sometimes reconfigured, usually because the advertisements were fluid. Two senior women journalists had also returned to TOI and were assisting him with these issues.

One particularly harried afternoon, Darryl was tearing out his non-existent hair, realizing he would have to revert to earlier layouts. He hollered at his secretary, "Where are the two old dummies?" And the redoubtable Unni replied, "They've gone for lunch."

...NEW LEARNINGS

We learnt not from orders, but by example. The Jains were doing all this themselves too.

For two of the young members of Delhi Response team helping Nandita Jain in her grand celebration, the sesquicentennial was something of a personal leap. Said Indira Deish, "We would get up at 4 am to be at the Morning Ragas event by 5.30 sharp, We would be lined up, dressed in auspicious traditional Indian colours, to sprinkle rose water on the guests. We socialised a lot and we learnt the nuances of hospitality, how to welcome and look after guests till the time they left. We learnt not from orders, but by example. The Jains were doing all this themselves too."

Teena Singh recalled, "For us, the 150-years events were a cultural awakening. We were in our early 20s, and came from backgrounds where we had never been exposed to such a high level of music, dance – and fashion. And here we were actually involved with the show of Yves St Laurent himself or the legends as Sting, Bruce Springstein and Tracy Chapman. Where would we ever have had such an opportunity before – or even later? It was mind-blowing for us. And it gave us an early and instant rooting into the Jain family and the TOI in a way that would have taken years, if at all."

VIBES GOOD & BAD

*It is sometimes the saboteur,
subverting archaic laws and pomposities.
It fuels aspiration unabashedly.*

The Jains, especially Samir and Indu-ji, have put the company on a path not usually trodden by media barons. In fact, the flagship Times of India appears to be sitting under The Speaking Tree, internalizing and propagating meta-corporate philosophies. It is not just the sutradhar of news, or the Chanakya of the political court, or even the indignant flag waver. Far from it. The paper chooses to play the jester or provides the spangled circus to distract from depressive times. It puts disaster in perspective and, dealing with the death toll in one sentence, goes on to elevate the soul with survivor stories and those extolling the human spirit. It is sometimes the saboteur, subverting archaic laws and pomposities. It fuels aspiration unabashedly.

It follows that decisions are not made on the basis of business alone. Even in the matter of a painting. When the Times Bank office opened at the street level of the Times of India building on Mumbai's DN Road, its most magnetic feature was Tyeb Mehta's massive canvas, 'Mahishasura'. The bank shut down after a while. The Tyeb continued to soar in value, but the Jains sold it because Samir's friend and art connoisseur Harsh Goenka said it emanated overpowering negative vibes. It was put on the block at Christie's in September 2002, and achieved the highest price ever of an Indian painting on a per sq inch basis: $107,550. The Jains knew that the canvas would be worth an even more astronomical sum, and climbing, as the years went by. But, there was a reason to sever ties with it, and there are no regrets.

VIBES GOOD & BAD

...'Get the finest suiting material available'.

FOLLOW SUIT

Among the diverse tasks assigned to Ashok Sen, one was to oversee the sartorial grooming of Vijay Jindal, then fast-tracking his way to the powerful triumvirate which also included PG and Arun Arora. Samir Jain's instruction was 'Get the finest suiting material available'. Then Ashok would take him to his master-cutter at 'Appearances', Delhi's best-known tailoring boutique. The evening would be rounded off with Jindal taking Ashok to Madhushala, the bar at the National Sports Club of India.

TIMELESS ART

Obviously money is not a factor for this cash-rich group. The decision to put parts of its collection up for auction was to create a buzz in the international market.

The group's art footprint is arguably Nandita Jain's most enduring legacy. Today paintings and some sculptures worth several crores are dispersed over several properties across offices, guesthouses and the family's homes.

On September 16, 2009, the group put one of its J Swaminathans up for auction at Christie's; it fetched $530,500 (`2.65 crore). It was a 1991 untitled oil and wax canvas, part of a series of 20 commissioned by BCCL in its endeavour to introduce art into work places. The first of this series was sold in March 2004 for $77,675 (`37,28,000), and the second in December 2004 for $1,00,000 (`48,00,000). The money from the sale of the masters goes to support promising young artists.

Some auction sales caused heartburn. Ashok Sen, who is the art curator of the Times Group along with his Response department hat, pulled out one of his bulging files of correspondence and clippings, and leafed through the dog-eared sheaf to locate an anguished letter from Gulam Sheikh to Samir Jain in September 4, 2004.

Several years ago the group had commissioned Gulam and his wife Nilima Sheikh, an equally sought-after artist, to execute six panels for the exalted 4th floor of Delhi's Times House where the top brass sits. But subsequently it was decided to put one of them, titled 'Between Memory and Music', under the hammer.

Gulam objected to the dismantling of the panels, saying that it 'dismembers what was meant to be a single work'. Below the letter, the VC's spidery crawl had noted: 'A Sen. Please decide. If not sent, you can withdraw. If sent, you can raise price or send all 6 as a group. Sabina may advise if there are implications.'

Ashok Sen flipped a few sheets to arrive at his own reply to Gulam: 'An overseas auction creates a benchmark for the artists and collectors as well … The intention is never to dismantle or dismember, but to create wealth with all available resources. We strongly believe that the value of the works commissioned by Nanditaji and put out by you can only appreciate in this manner and this is the only way forward to put Indian art on a global pedestal. We have loved every moment of our ownership of these works, and would now love to give back to the artist fraternity a global recognition whereby their names would be discussed alongside the names of the better known masters.' Indeed, this was the first time that a Ghulam was sold in an international auction. Sen decided against the VC's alternative of selling all six at one go because that 'would have devalued each of them'.

The group began selling internationally in 1999, with KK Hebbar's 'Kite flying' at Christie's in London.

Obviously money is not a factor for this cash-rich group. The decision to put parts of its collection up for auction was to create a buzz in the international market.

Sen's files reveal that the group has another view when it comes to loaning out its works. Rajiv Lochan, director of Delhi's National Gallery of Modern Art, had approached him when the NGMA was organising a Retrospective of KG Subramanyan. Sen had replied saying that corporate collectors should not be asked. 'It is difficult for us to monitor movement and adequate insurance while on the move. (We have insurance while it is on our properties).'

TIMELESS ART

It's not just paintings and sculpture. Dileep Padgaonkar, the Executive Editor, bought an entire lot of 39 old film posters which had come on the market, and they were all displayed on the Times of India editorial floor in Delhi. It was a rare archive of popular culture. In 2003, the company decided to dispose of them. They were all picked up – by Dileep himself, who by then had left the company.

And here's another manifestation of Samir Jain's generosity."Senior managers have been overwhelmed to see him arrive personally bearing an expensive canvas. Mahendra Swaroop was 'deeply touched' when VC gifted him a Thomas Easley in 2003.

Incidentally, Easley was the artist who did the pop-iconography on the façade of Delhi's Times House, the Krishna legend in poster colours and comic book style which became such a traffic stopper, and exploded the grey of Delhi's Fleet Street, Bahadurshah Zafar Marg.

*Yet, over the decades,
the Times of India's landmark building
on Mumbai's DN Road has managed,
more or less, to keep its dignity
safe from the molestation
that goes by the name of modernisation.*

FACING THE MUSIC

Is art only what you put up on walls, or install in public spaces? Does heritage have to be at least a hundred years old to merit conservation? Must milestones from one era in corporate history be turned into paving blocks when a later army marches up to claim its stake?

A company as old and as new as Bennett Coleman has to grapple with these questions as a matter of routine. You cannot date back to the early 19th century plus be ahead of the 21st, and not expect scores of totems from even the recent past to become vulnerable to the Next Big Thing.

Yet, over the decades, the Times of India's landmark building on Mumbai's DN Road has managed, more or less, to keep its dignity safe from the molestation that goes by the name of modernisation. Its original innocuous entrance was remodeled only to complement not compete with the grand façade.

The interiors had been modified many times to keep up with changing and growing needs. The most definitive make-over came during the 150th jubilee in 1988-89 to reflect the conscious change in the company's relationship with readers and advertisers. Even then, the Old Lady of Bori Bunder may have thrown away her corset, and emerged in a designer bustier, but she did not abandon the mainstays of her support, physical or figurative.

FACING THE MUSIC

The instructions to the interiors architect were unambiguous and non-negotiable: the cast-iron pillars had to remain, not just because they were a structural necessity, but because they held up history. Vocabulary could be jazzed up, but grammar is sacrosanct. Subsequent remodeling remained faithful to this rule.

However, a monumental destruction took place in 2008 just as the year was ready to lay its terrorised ghosts. The 'enemy within' did not subvert surreptitiously. No, the worrying part was that the change went past all the sanctioning procedures which are the checks and balances of the corporate machine. Even more ironically, it wasn't some deadwood of the company's 19th-century past which got axed to make way for a highway to the future. The victim of the hatchet job was its most recent showpiece: the funky, over-the-top entertainment floor, specifically the domain of Times Music.

Nearly a decade after the upheaval of the sesquicentennial, a high-decibel revolution had overpowered the fourth floor's newer wing. Where once-crusty librarians had prowled amid musty clippings, an 'underwater fantasy' exploded in 1997. It was a well-thought-out and audaciously executed act of iconoclasm. The ambience had been created to smash the staid idol of the Old Lady of Bori Bunder and replace it with that of a Spice Girl. It was another inflexion point, marking the group's mediamorphosis from conventional print to splashy, flashy entertainment.

You entered the Times Music and later Zoom offices through a riveted metal tunnel, it was like boarding the Beatles' Yellow Submarine, only this one was blue. Clever work-stations served both privacy and interaction, the twin needs of the creative process. To charge it up, or vent steam, there was a large abacus in the passage, and a convex mirror in which you could go make faces – or reflect upon altered reality. Fish tanks heightened the serendipity, and the ceiling was festooned with nets.

Creativity was not to be disturbed, so visitors were not allowed in the main hall, but instead were zapped into cheeky meeting rooms, the discussion tables progressively shaped like LPs, cassettes and DVDs to symbolize the march of music's ritualistic receptacles. Reflecting the growth and success of BCCL's media and entertainment empire, a larger conference room bubbled up, its portholes abloom with neon-coloured scrunches.

It was the closest thing that commerce had to installation art, and it was the furthest look imaginable from the long - perceived face of the Times Group. It won hallelujahs from design Valhallas.

But one day – poof! – it was all gone. All the thought, effort and audacity that had been invested in it disappeared because of one numbing failure. Someone failed to recognise it for what it was, a milestone in BCCL's march into the future, and saw it only as a tool of administrative expediency. The *Mumbai Mirror*'s expansion plans demanded more space, and this was the nearest chunk at hand. An iconoclastic icon was felled, not to table a point, but to install a set of chairs.

...an 'underwater fantasy' exploded in 1997. It was a well-thought-out and audaciously executed act of iconoclasm.

An enraged Samir Jain called it a 'desecration', and likened it to the Agra municipality demolishing the Taj Mahal to make room for burgeoning traffic. 'Atonement' was demanded, and submitted. Then, from the debris of the Times Music Room rose a revised set of systems and processes which would enshrine why what was where it was, and why it should remain unsavaged by ignorant armies.

As in all mythology, destruction and creation are merely the flip sides of each other.

PRAFUL, WHO?

"To which party do you belong?"

He may have headed an empire that could make or break governments and politicians, but Samir Jain was never interested in politics. When he met Praful Patel, albeit not yet the high-flying minister for civil aviation, he indiscreetly asked "To which party do you belong?" It caused considerable embarrassment to Pradeep Guha who had introduced him, and who certainly didn't share his boss's lack of interest in the power that flows from the barrel of political office.

Guha revelled in the story of how often the Shiv Sena's trenchant 'Supremo' called him to tell him what should or should not have gone into the TOI of which Pradeep was then Director in charge. "So, one day I told him, 'Balasaheb, why don't you simply come and sit in my chair?"

FAIR GAME

The latest is a Feel Free Committee, the initiative of the chairman, Indu Jain, herself.

Sexual harassment is an occupational hazard for women, as well as for the management in any organisation. Sometimes personnel managers themselves have been too up close and personal by any standards of decency. Even editors, high on the aphrodisiac – and invulnerability – of power have leered, made lewd remarks or suggestions, but have wisely drawn the line at any forced sex. The Times has instituted a succession of measures to remove the humiliation which sadly exists even for feisty women reporters who are flag-bearers of gender justice. The latest is a Feel Free Committee, the initiative of the chairman, Indu Jain, herself.

Long before this, the medical room had a groping doctor. The women marched in a delegation to the GM, Dr Ram Tarneja. He gave them a polite hearing. But they had to go three times before the fellow was removed. A woman doctor was appointed for the pre-lunch shift.

Several TOI office romances had 'lived happily ever after' endings.

EXTRA MARITAL ARRANGEMENTS

Several TOI office romances had 'lived happily ever after' endings. But some were distinctly non-kosher which added an edge to the affair, and spice for the salivating observers. The sidelined wife, of course, was a different kettle in these fishy tales.

The suave head of RMD was having a flaming affair with one of his executives, adding pleasure to their 'business' trips together. It was BCCL's worst-kept secret. But then a zealous accountant scrutinised the chief's hotel bills. A double breakfast could be explained as entertaining a dealer or contact, but lingerie in the laundry bill could not slip past as easily. Questions were raised, not just eyebrows. A head rolled, and as is the discriminatory corporate practice, it was that of the woman subordinate.

But this came later. Nemesis and the man's wife had arrived earlier when he was visiting Bangalore. The Mrs came along with him to the local office. While she was there, The Other Woman kept calling, and the secretary of the Branch head, unfamiliar with the goings-on, kept telling her that the boss was in a meeting.

On the nth call, the tired secretary asked, "Who should I say is calling?" The mistress said, "Tell him it's his sister." The secretary went in and said, "Sir, there's a lady on the line for you." The man hastily said, "I'll take it outside." As soon as he stepped out, the suspicious wife demanded, "Who's call is it?" The secretary innocently replied, "His sister's." And got the tart response, "He doesn't have one."

WHEN TATA SAID BYE-BYE

Egos were bruised,
slights were imagined,
corporate decorum was deemed breached,
and it all snowballed with tit for tata.

The Times Group and the Tatas got into a long drawn-out but quiet spat in the mid-2000s. Egos were bruised, slights were imagined, corporate decorum was deemed breached, and it all snowballed with tit for tata. From an inconsequential beginning it grew into a cold war where the Economic Times was covertly accused of being biased against the Tatas and towards the Ambanis. The Tatas withdrew their advertising. Neither side blinked, each assuming that the other could not survive in the corporate jungle by quarreling with their own perceived lion.

BCCL satraps put pressure to black out the Tatas from editorial content. VC, master of the subtle rapier thrust, would have none of that. The grape-vine has it that a quantitative methodology was arrived at: for every four good stories, one negative story was permitted. Anything else would have gone against the very core of his belief that you need to be a happy paper.

MEDIA-NOT

It became a handy weapon for rivals to undermine the entire success of the TOI.

The TOI Group is the declared mass murderer of established media conventions. And revels in the reputation. One of the first instruments of slaughter was Medianet. The idea of selling editorial space in the supplements – in however controlled a fashion – came under huge attack not just in India, but also in international conferences. It became a handy weapon for rivals to undermine the entire success of the TOI.

In 2003, this chronicler gave a presentation on Measuring Editorial Quality at the Dublin conference of the World Editors Forum, using the TOI as the primary example. As soon as she finished, an Englishman in the first row creaked to his feet and pointedly asked, "But isn't yours the paper which has desecrated the sanctity of editorial space by selling it for PR and promotions?" She and her entire spiel lay shattered under this offensive in the presence of global peers. She did not have the nerve or the presence of mind to tell them what she had told PG some seven years earlier in a wider context.

Thanks to the group's gobsmacking business success, every meeting of journalists ended up being a confrontation of TOI vs the Rest. Fed up of one more senior staffer returning bloodied from this battle, PG, the director in charge, called me down to his office and suggested I give it back in my next weekly column. I told him, "No point. The Times is like a huge mango tree; small boys can't help throwing stones at it."

MEDIA-NOT

Several years later, the attack on Medianet had got so vicious that all five directors met at the Bombay Gym to formulate a response. They may not have heard this decade-old story, but the not-unanimous decision reached was a wise one. Do nothing. Just sit quiet.

It's different now. A couple of years after that, Ravi Dhariwal, by then CEO of the TOI, was invited as a speaker at a conference organised by the Asian Institute of Journalism in Chennai. The Hindu's N Murali and T N Ninan, once the star editor of ET, then with Business Standard, expectedly launched a blitzkrieg on Medianet and the TOI, but Dhariwal deftly turned the tables, not only defending the strategy and the company, but taking both into an unreachable high ground.

Do nothing. Just sit quiet.

Dhariwal was then still a comparative unknown in the media industry, but his speech created a huge wave within and outside the group. Some colleagues thought it was brilliant. Others darkly, and predictably, muttered that he shouldn't have been there at all.

In any event, many media houses have Medianet by other means. The difference is that they do it tucked away behind bushes, while BCCL does it as 'khullam khulla' as reckless lovers.

A few years after Medianet, BCCL obligingly handed its interlocutors another dagger dripping with the blood of editorial compromise. This was Private Treaties, by which BCCL barters its 'prime real estate' of space for equity in growing businesses and thus helps them to build their brand. If you want to know whom to blame, listen to Mahendra Swarup. His TIL set the tills ringing.

"When it started, Times Internet Ltd was a cash-strapped business of Bennett. Indiatimes would take a lot of space in BCCL's print media products since these were the best and, for us, the cheapest way of building our new brand. VC didn't like it. So one day, just off the cuff, I said, 'Why don't you charge me?' VC reached out for the intercom and in his usual way summoned half a dozen people, R Sundar, Sumanta Pal, etc. MD is seldom called into VC's room (and vice versa is never) but each brother expects those present to inform him of what has transpired."

From that chance dig, a gold-mine was created.

PARTY TIMES

"It had a Maru wedding look..."

The Bombay Times party would become the glitziest event of the Indian social calendar after the mid-90s, with Pradeep Guha displaying, and enhancing, his equity with the movers, shapers and swingers of urbane India. The glamorous BT editor, Malavika Sangghvi would be at his side in designer - bare. But in earlier regimes, what passed off as a successful party was really quite staid, if not dull.

The quintessential host Samir Jain didn't begin to throw party-parties till the very late '90s. They were usually held in one of the family residences, the food was lavish and multicultural, but always vegetarian, though egg subsequently slipped in via soufflés. However liquor was never served.

Dr Ram Tarneja, the high-network GM, didn't have to adhere to Jain House rules. His invitation always said 'Cocktails' (and Dinner, sometimes). Blended Scotch was de rigeur; the single malt fashion was still to hit the double peg. As for that other pretension, White and Red were then only Scotch whiskey labels.

At parties, no one ever saw Dr T with a full glass in his hand. It was always only half so, and he would slip it into his jacket pocket every time he had to shake a guest's hand, or even when he tired of holding it. When some other host asked him,"How's your drink?" he would pull out the whiskey tumbler, raise it, and say "Fine."

Pradeep Guha may have created the state of mind called The Bombay Times Party, but having left, he sniffed: "It had a Maru wedding look, with the family and senior directors lined up at the entrance to greet the guests. I thought it very uncool". Really?

VC, whose eyes miss nothing, has commented on the sudden disappearance of his guests, but has chosen to accept the proffered lie.

ONE FOR THE LOAD

Vineet Jain will crack a bottle of fine wine or even pop the champagne, but no alcohol is served at the VC's homes in Delhi or Mumbai. However, in Delhi, which is his base, watering-holes are conveniently situated next door.

So it is not unusual for editors or even directors or managers to have a quick one at the Taj Man Singh whose back gate is across the road from Sujagi. When the whole family was still staying at Jain House on SP Marg, Hotel Diplomat, three bungalows down the road provided the necessary lubrication.

Sometimes, even a hasty nip from a bottle kept in the car parked outside was resorted to. VC, whose eyes miss nothing, has commented on the sudden disappearance of his guests, but has chosen to accept the proffered lie.

ONE FOR THE LOAD

VI

the family ways

"But myth is something else than an explanation of the world, of history, and of destiny."

– Paul Ricoeur –

PARIVAR INC

However, you are never far from a reminder that BCCL is a small, closely meshed family, not a formidable corporation.

All the shareholder Jains must be referred to not by their name-jis, but by their designations: Chairman, VC, MD for Indu, Samir and Vineet, respectively. However, you are never far from a reminder that BCCL is a small, closely meshed family, not a formidable corporation.

In the early years of MD's official entry into the business, he came into the Directors' Lunch Room in Mumbai straight from the airport. His mother, who had been camping in this city for some weeks and hadn't seen her younger son in a while, simply strolled up to him, and planted a maternal kiss on his cheek. The senior managers and editors present may have been startled but they remembered to smile indulgently.

If the Chairman is in town during one of VC's agenda-setting or game-changing discourses to senior management and editorial, she will have been informed of this meeting, and she will glide in serenely, dressed in her signature flowing style, her skin glowing. Her meticulously laid-out tea will arrive next, multi-grain toast, slim bottles of sugar-free, whole-fruit French jam. A secretary will ceremonially pour out her fresh-squeezed juice or herbal brew or both.

Chairman, in all likelihood, will walk over to VC with a plate of spread toast, and place it before him as naturally as if this were the intimate family table, not the intimidating infinity of Burma teak. VC will not touch it.

The cut and dried MD is never part of these elaborate, seemingly rambling rituals.

Nothing denotes Parivar Inc as clearly as the fact that all family residences segue into company guest houses for senior managers and editors. There are no cordoned-off sections marked 'Private'

VC insists on visiting directors and editors staying at his own Delhi home, Sujagi, instead of the other guesthouses. He will arrive with an extra razai on a cold winter night, or with a tea tray early in the morning, and request them to join him for his walk around the manicured grounds as he expounds on some newly inspired thought.

Once, Mahendra Swarup was invited to a meeting with the family's three-generational ladies. They spent two hours with him, being the most gracious hostesses and, along the way, advising him, as VC's mother, wife and daughter, respectively. Chairperson Indu-ji told him that "VC, even as a boy, insisted on a certain pattern of interaction". Mrs Samir Jain, Meera said, "He likes to be kept informed not only on what you are doing, but also why." And Trishla came up with her own take on 'Dealing with Papa'.

The ex-MNC honcho recalled, "In no other company would a professional manager get such a personalised, 360-degree input on his boss."

WHEN THE CHAIRMAN IS A WOMAN

'Chair-Prasanna'

The luminously beautiful Indu Jain was named Chairman after her husband's death in Cleveland on February 4, 1999, following a heart transplant. Managers and editors resigned themselves to coping with one more mercurial set of personal traits. In its early avatar, the board on her office door read 'Chair-Prasanna'; it later reverted to the more conventional term.

In the first months, Indu-ji called frequent meetings to convey her concept of what the

TOI publications should be. She wanted a kinder, gentler, happier paper – which stunned the conventional dispensers of doom and disaster, gloom and gore. She imposed a ban on negative stories about contemporary gurus since these would wound their countless followers. Again jaws dropped and heads shook in disbelief because godmen had come to be more associated with scams than sanctity, and provided daily grist to the media mill.

But over the years, from this has been distilled the positive approach to the daily dose of calamity – the emphasis on the spark of human goodness which elevates all tragedy. Readers have embraced this enthusiastically.

Indu Jain has also brought her own stamp to the way she conducts her meetings, using the clout of the TOI – and her own determination, charm and girlish enthusiasm.

Indu Jain has also brought her own stamp to the way she conducts her meetings, using the clout of the TOI – and her own determination, charm and girlish enthusiasm – to get the good, the great and the materialistically selfish to pitch their wherewithal into her pet causes. These are the environment, peace, education and, most effective of all, 'saha-bhagi', people power as a joint and active stakeholder in government and municipal decision-making.

The Times Foundation is her baby. A space has been carved out in the Mumbai TOI building for free classes on anything from reiki to the *Rig Veda*. In Delhi, after Nandita's passing, the entire Lutyens bungalow on 4, Tilak Marg has been made over to holistic well-being, services for the public.

A great believer in the power of Shakti, Indu Jain once called a meeting of Mumbai's mover and shaker women to discuss how their collective inner force could be used to unleash the greater good. Some of them fidgeted awkwardly when the meeting began – as all those of Indu-ji do – with

WHEN THE CHAIRMAN IS A WOMAN

everyone expected to produce the reverberation of the cosmic 'Aum'. Then a bowl of flowers arrived 'charged with positive energy' as a gift for Ananya Goenka,who had just been appointed Chairperson of the Indian Express Group.

Yes, like Maggi, Indu Mata is different. And, yes, she can be saucy too.

Eggs were subsequently introduced at Sujagi, but only the whites – that made it kosher enough since 'life' was in the yolk.

POHA, PROFITS AND PURANAS

As we said, all the Jain family residences in Delhi and Mumbai double as guesthouses for visiting senior staff. The food is prepared with the care of a private home, and is, of course, vegetarian.

Breakfast is usually poha healthified with vegetables, stuffed toasties, idli or dosa with sambar. There is always an appropriate chutney, freshly ground. Eggs were subsequently introduced at Sujagi, but only the whites – that made it kosher enough since 'life' was in the yolk.

Incidentally, all the three establishments in South Delhi's crucible of privilege are referred to as 'Chhey number' (6, SP Marg), 'Char number' (4, Tilak Marg) and 'Pandrah number' (15, Motilal Nehru Marg), though, on the VC's constant tutoring, the last-mentioned is called by its proper, well-thought-out name, Sujagi. It means 'self awakening'. It has in fact become an extension of the office on Bahadurshah Zafar Marg.

POHA, PROFITS AND PURANAS

When Bangalore's *Vijay Karnataka* was being bought over by BCCL in 2006, Ravi Dhariwal had been locked in price negotiations with the founder Vijay Sankeshwar at Delhi's The Oberoi till 10 pm, too late and too tired to make the long drive back to his farm house in Chhatarpur. So Dhariwal decided to sleep over at Sujagi which is only 10 mins away from The Oberoi. "VC came into my room at 5.30 am, and we walked for an hour and a half in the dawn garden. He gave all the needed approvals. By noon we had inked the deal."

Personally understated,
she brought in a style not seen
before in the TOI.

DIYA IN THE WIND

The late Nandita Jain was bubbly, committed, humane and, like her older brother Samir, overwhelmingly generous.

Personally understated, she brought in a style not seen before in the TOI. The Lutyens bungalow on 4, Tilak Marg was given to her when she married, but the ET's 25th anniversary party was held here before she had transformed the classic but rundown property into a classy home with her sense of design and enviable art collection.

The lawn was tatty, but in a week she had got in the bulldozers to level and lay it with 1ft x1ft squares of grass bought from a supplier of such instant lushness.

An NDMC contractor created a glade in salmon pink, the paper's colour. This was achieved by bandaging the trees in crepe ribbon, and cleverly using papered spotlights. An exporter friend of a friend supplied pink damask napkins. Pink champagne was served.

DIYA IN THE WIND

The blush was of pride at the magical effect. It was talked about for months, as much internally. As one of the core team put it in characteristic droll manner, "You must remember that in those days we were still very stingy. The company was not given to what Delhiites call 'show-sha'." The family still isn't.

Nandita Jain was fully engaged in the business. She introduced the now globally acclaimed Newspapers in Education programme. She brought colour into the TOI. She spearheaded the yearlong sesquicentennial celebrations with love, zeal and imagination. During that time she was the force behind turning the drab Times of India buildings in Mumbai and Delhi into Wow workspaces.

"You must remember that in those days we were still very stingy. The company was not given to what Delhiites call 'show-sha'." The family still isn't.

She travelled to Shekhawati in Rajasthan to buy the latticed jharokas which adorn the Response office in Mumbai. Among her most inspired ideas for the Delhi Response cabins was to stick the zinc plates of the old printing process onto plywood, and turn them into sliding doors for the floor-to-ceiling storage cabinets.

She wasn't just the owner's daughter holding a token position, and sashaying in and out. She was hands-on, up to her elbows in fact, in everything she took on.

One of these was the Advertising, later-Response department. Teena Singh and Indira Deish remembered how, in the early days when they were handling the Hindi publications, both would companionably go on calls together to the same place and person. Nandita, who checked the daily reports meticulously, soon caught this duplication of time and effort, and put an end to it.

But she was a friendly boss. She took her team out for lunch and dinner regularly, and, unlike her brothers, expected to be called by her first name.

Nandita was always ready to give reward where due. Indira and Teena, bright-eyed and bushy-tailed, would bring in a record number of bookings. In their second year, in 1985, they were given six increments each. Which wasn't as Whoopee-worthy as it seemed because, in their grade, each jump was '30. So this added up to just '180 – before tax.

"We barged into our boss's room, and whined, 'Nandita, everyone says Excellent, Excellent, but we've only got six increments.' 'What!' she exclaimed, and immediately took our increment letters and noted in her neat hand, 'Plus Four', signing the correction with an 'NJ'." It was a simpler time.

Nandita was a maverick in many ways. Untypically, she numbered TOI journalists among her close, personal friends: the inhouse couple, Shikha Trivedi and SP Singh, Pritish Nandy and Sabina Sehgal Saikia.

Art was Nandita's grand passion. She studied the subject and the market closely. Sabina and Shikha were her help-mates in this. Together they built the group's formidable collection. Nandita was the reason why 'Timeless Art' was the awesome, gawk-some opening act of the sesquicentennial celebrations in Mumbai. It was overseen by the renowned artist, Manjit Bawa, and all the panels were assembled in Delhi at 4, Tilak Marg.

Pritish was her righthand man for this in Mumbai, and Sabina and Shikha worked closely with her on the Delhi events, especially the classical music and dance.

DIYA IN THE WIND

S P, who later became the star news anchor of Aaj Tak, died in his 30s of a cerebral stroke on June 28, 1997. Sabina, in her 40s, fell to the 26/11 terrorist attack on the Taj Mahal Hotel in 2008. Their vivacious friend also met a premature end. On May 10, 2001, the Pawan Hans chopper carrying Nandita Jain and seven others crashed into the forests of Arunachal where she had gone to set up a school under the aegis of for her beloved guru, Sri Sri Ravi Shankar.

A photograph of Nandita, exuberant and alive, beams from a wall in Vineet's Delhi office (as it does from the two other offices she had occupied at Times House). Nothing could soften the blow of the loss of his confident, caring sister.

LITTLE BLACK NOTEBOOK

"It's just his way of telling you that you should take down detailed notes."

In low-tech times, it was almost an act of high treason not to arrive at one of VC's durbars without a writing pad. A senior editor newly inducted to the high table was flattered when one of the directors handed her an elegant little notebook clad in red Chinese brocade saying, "This is a gift from VC." She preeningly told PG about it, who promptly brought her down to earth with "It's just his way of telling you that you should take down detailed notes."

Now the notebooks have been replaced by laptops – VC likes them as much as he abhors cell phones. The former 'focus your energies' instead of the latter's distracting intrusions. When they are in Delhi, both brothers often operate out of their separate floors of Sujagi, and managers all arrive bearing their PCs, and immediately flip them open as they alert themselves for an hour or, in the case of VC, a whole morning (and evening).

LITTLE BLACK NOTEBOOK

Occasionally, VC summons the senior managers and editors to the formidable 3rd floor Mumbai boardroom with its long Burma teak table and heritage mahogany paneling to apprise them of some new philosophy (it's never a 'strategy') that will take the paper's content to yet the next level. In Delhi, the 4th floor DLR doubles as the boardroom.

The meeting will always be somewhat surreal since VC will give an insightful and awesomely informed discourse. It might start with a Samurai treatise, wander into pre-Raphaelite art, and end with the symbolism behind the 'cultivated Mafiosi look' of celebrities. VC never issues direct instructions on how to shape editorial. It is always elliptical, always lateral, the sweep of knowledge always so fascinating that you can get mesmerised. And lose sight of the fundamental objective. That is a lapse as unforgivable as not busily taking down notes.

The family is not exempt. If they are in town and in the office, they will be invited. The Chairman naturally has a secretary doing this for her, but VC's daughter Trishla, who is being inducted into the business, and even his wife, Meera, who is not really a part of it, jot their take-aways from the VC's tour de force.

One morning,
DMD pointed out that
the masthead of Business Times
was a millimeter deeper
than it should have been.
He had actually measured it.

DEVIL IN THE DETAILS

Vineet Jain's style is to look at the minute details because these are where God (and the devil) reportedly resides. When the Bangalore edition was being turned around, he was Deputy Managing Director, DMD. As the consulting editor stationed there, I would get a call like clockwork with the daily check list. This would be relayed by his lieutenant in Delhi, Sumanta Pal, whom the irritated Bangalore RE had labeled DDMD. Pronounced with emphatic sarcasm – Dee-Dee-Em-Dee!

One morning, DMD pointed out that the masthead of *Business Times* was a millimeter deeper than it should have been. He had actually measured it.

When a new design or masthead is being planned, Vineet Jain, now the MD, gets scores of options, lays them out on the table, and summons people from across the empire – Internet, Brand, Response, RMD, Editorial – to choose the 'best' one. Finally, he calls in his trusted PA, Ganga Nair. He is the sure-fire sounding board because "If it is relevant to Ganga, it's bound to be relevant to the people out there."

DEVIL IN THE DETAILS

The MD is totally clued in to what will excite the end-user, especially new media consumers. The tipping point for Times Now came with its carpet bombing coverage of the rescue of Prince, the little boy trapped in a Kurukshetra borewell for 48 hours. Vineet Jain was at the other end of the ear-piece of the anchor, Arnab Goswami, upping the ante by telling him to flood the screen with viewer reactions. Arnab would later describe it thus: "It was as if the entire nation was waiting to have its say on this tragedy – and triumph. MD sensed it, and made us give it full play."

BLOW HOT, BLOW COOL

It had to be neither too formal nor too flippant.

The MD who took the group into the sequined strobe-lights of new media is innately shy. Over the years, he has learnt to deliver a perfectly pitched argument at a conclave, but the late and much-missed Sabina Sehgal Saikia once recounted the agony he went through while preparing his short speech for the launch of the Indian '*Hello!*' It is part of Worldwide Media, BCCL's magazines joint venture with the BBC.

Sabina coaxed, coached and corrected MD for 30 minutes, each saying 'Hello!' over and over again till he had achieved the exact emphasis he wanted in the two syllables, the precise balance in the exclamation mark. It had to be neither too formal nor too flippant.

Yet, at an inhouse celebration, he not just gamely but most enthusiastically strutted his stuff. He walked down the ramp at the 'fashion show', stylishly twirling his leather jacket in the air, while his 'partner', Delhi's Resident Editor, froze right down to her bone marrow in her backless, sequined, Ritu Kumar choli on that bitterly cold winter night out in the open of a Chhatarpur farmhouse.

We are always giving instructions, but we are too superior to lift a hand and do even the smallest job ourselves.

DIY DEEDS

When Samir Jain was a very young man, still living in the marble pile of Jain House on Calcutta's millionaire mile of Alipore, he stopped short during his usual morning walk around the extensive grounds. Someone had scrawled into the dust on the window of the guard's cabin, 'Sheesha saaf karna hai'. The lad said to his companion, "This is the major failing of our people. We are always giving instructions, but we are too superior to lift a hand and do even the smallest job ourselves." He then pulled out a handkerchief and wiped the glass clean.

MEDIA GLARE, GLARINGLY ABSENT

Ringmasters simply don't feel the need to be part of the social circus. One is a notoriously lonely number.

Neither Samir nor Vineet Jain will be seen holding the stage at global or Indian media- industry forums. Their second line of command, notably Ravi Dhariwal from around 2007, are the members of organizations such as the World Association of Newspapers or INMA. Both brothers are actually uncomfortable in public appearances, and will never ever be seen working a party crowd. They will make the necessary appearance if they want to or have to, and then make a quick exit.

They prefer going with the 'air cover' of a coterie to bail them out of awkward social moments, or help them along with a political fellow guest. This might seem odd considering that their papers can make or break any of these strutting party animals. The truth could be that having made a principle, even a virtue, of distance, they really don't want to get co-opted by familiarity.

Besides, ringmasters simply don't feel the need to be part of the social circus. One is a notoriously lonely number.

GENEROUS WITH A 'J'

"Yeh aap ke liye, aur yeh aap ke liye."

Generosity is the distinguishing trait of Samir Jain as it was of his late sister, Nandita. Every time, either of them returned from abroad, they would come bearing expensive gifts.

One morning, VC walked into Arun Arora's room, where Pradeep Guha was also sitting, with a carrier bag. Pulling out two boxes, he said, "Yeh aap ke liye, aur yeh aap ke liye." They were Gucci shoes. Then to their joint disbelief, he proceeded to bend down and put them on for Guha, who was as mortified as touched. "I could have died," he recalled.

To this day Arora hasn't figured out, "But how did he know our exact sizes?" It's a question asked by all recipients of his largesse, whether it is bespoke French shirts or designer belts.

One day, while waiting in Ashok Jain's office in Delhi, Guha had stood admiring a table clock, a replica of the famed Dali soft clock. The meeting with the Chairman and Samir Jain over, he left to catch his flight back to Mumbai. As he was getting into the lift, a peon came scurrying up with a hastily wrapped packet, and said, "VC sahib ne yeh bheja hai." It was the clock.

Samir Jain was so excited over his 'baby' brother Vineet's wedding, that he came over with two suit lengths each for Arora and Guha. He personally took Arun to his own tailor, giving precise instructions on its style and trimmings.

And some weeks after Ashok Jain had passed away in Cleveland from complications arising after a heart transplant, the VC came to Arora with a bagful of clothes. He said, "Papa loved you very much. He would have liked you to have some of his favourite things." It included a classic white bow tie which Arora hasn't had the occasion – nor summoned the gumption – to wear. But it remains his treasured possession.

Knowing his taste for distinctive objets d'art, and objets de provocateur, Nandita gave Guha a heavily worked Asian antique silver box. Closer examination revealed the engravings to be erotic figures.

Nandita's husband, the businessman Amit Judge, had acquired the franchise for Lacoste. One afternoon after a meeting, she took the Response executives to a room piled with these 'alligator shirts', and said, "Help yourself." Everyone enthusiastically did. It was an order from the boss, no?

Nandita was always simply dressed, usually in just a white salwar kurta, but the flamboyant Sabina Sehgal Saikia, her friend and collaborator, often spoke of how she would return after a trip to Mumbai and thrust upon her an armful of dramatic saris from Vama or other exclusive store.

Like a good north Indian
he had also brought along
an emergency ration of matthi,
so they made do
with this snack for breakfast.

BREAKFAST & TIFFINESE

In the unliberalized world of P forms and absurd forex restrictions, the entitlement for foreign travel was abstemious. When Ramesh Chandra Jain and Arun Arora went to Paris to buy the Harris Heat-set Offset machine which would change not just the fortunes of the TOI, but the way all national newspapers would be printed, the director's allowance was $80 a day and that of the Modernisation head, $60.

They could have managed. But Samir Jain decided to accompany them, and insisted that they all stay in the same hotel. He was booked at the Marriott, and the rate was $140 a night. Too embarrassed to explain the financial predicament, Ramesh-ji and Arora had no option but to pool the sum total of their allowances, and share a room.

Bad enough, but Ramesh-ji couldn't start his day without bed tea, so he ordered room service, and paled at the bill. He paid for it from the clandestine dollars a friend had given him to buy some chocolates. Like a good north Indian he had also brought along an emergency ration of matthi, so they made do with this snack for breakfast. Lunch was with the vendor, and in the evening they were certain that Samir Jain would take them some place, and that it would be fancy.

When they met in the lobby, Samir asked what they'd had for breakfast. Arora breezily said, "Oh it was something in French, very good it was too." But the boss, in his usual curious way, asked for details, and the more the hungry duo tried to bluff, the more they tied themselves up in croissants.

The next morning, there was a knock on the door, and outside stood Samir Jain in a bathrobe, holding a laden tray. He said, "Meera, as usual, over-ordered, so I thought I should bring you all this extra food before you went down to breakfast."

The next day, he was at the door again, this time fully dressed, but again with a tray. The third day, a room service waiter did the needful.

There were many incidents which deepened the special bond between PG and Samir Jain. But in a crowded and impressive list, one stands out. "When my father died, VC arrived the same night from Delhi, and came straight from the airport to my Bandra flat. He had carried a large tiffin carrier with him and handed it to me saying matter-of-factly, 'You all must not have cooked or eaten anything since morning'."

Little wonder then that, several years after he left, PG stated with uncharacteristic emotion, "For me, the TOI was only the Response Department and Samir Jain."

The participants not only wallowed in VC's generosity, they also learnt about cost consciousness from him.

COST CAUSE

On the international Response conferences – holidays really – the participants not only wallowed in VC's generosity, they also learnt about cost consciousness from him. Once Indira Deish, while taking her room key, instructed the receptionist to give her a wake up call, and send a pot of bed tea with it. She felt a tap on her shoulder, turned around and saw VC. "He put his hand into his suit pocket, pulled out something, and put it in my palm. It was a couple of tea bags. After that, I always carried a box of these, and ordered only hot water. I learnt the value of thrift."

Much earlier, Indira learnt a similar lesson during the sesquicentennial celebrations in Delhi where she was part of the reception team. At the accompanying dinners, Samir Jain taught us "never to change a plate mid-meal. It unnecessarily added to the caterer's bill." Indira said, "This has become so ingrained in me that, at weddings, I never change the plate, aware that it would cost the host another Rs 2,000. I cringe when I see parents handing even small children a separate one."

Thrift lesson #3 came from a regular office advice. Samir Jain, preempting the later global fashion, sent detailed instructions on how to recycle, reuse, and refuse to waste. He made it into a 'criminal offence' to send a fax on a letterhead. The 'grains' pixelation of the printed header added three minutes more to the transmission time; so it was far more economical to photocopy and then fax. This became a 'best practice' at the Times.

Long before it became government policy under UPA II, austerity was the pride and joy of the TOI, or at least the fatwa of the VC – which some may say is the same thing. If you wrote a note to him, you made sure that you tore out the white space on the page to show that you weren't wasting paper. When he replied, it would certainly not be on some Ivorycote, monogrammed letterhead or even a memo pad. It would be on the back of your note.

Ashok Sen, Assistant VP, Response, mentioned another pointer to VC's cost sensitivity. With millions-worth of decisions on his mind, he spent a surprising amount of time to initiate senior managers into the art of routing business travel. He said, "You leave it to secretaries who are ill-equipped to handle ticketing from a cost perspective." Sen proceeded to pull out a fat file with mails on different routing options, and the VC's notes on fare permutations.

The VC's directive is 'Don't fly the cheapest class but fly the cheapest route.' This rule applies even to his family's travels. He goes into details on how a ticket is routed and what a flier can do en route within the same price. Ashok Sen recalled sitting with an atlas to see where VC could get a free stop when he first flew the Pacific route to the US. "I came up with Tahiti, and he loved the insights it gave him into the intricacies of Polynesian culture."

On domestic flights Samir Jain always traveled Economy. Vikas Singh, later Resident Editor in Delhi and a VC favourite, described the time he went with him to Mumbai. "We were held up at his satsang, drove like crazy to the airport, but we were still horrendously late, and were the last to board. The passengers already strapped in glowered at me, and looked sideways at VC, who

COST CAUSE

slyly winked at me. We were in Economy, and, as soon as the seatbelt sign went off, the high and the mighty began trooping down from the upper end to chat him up. Soon a jam began to form in the aisle.

"I asked him why he didn't simply travel in Business, and make things easier for everyone. He replied, 'I know elite products are about branding and marketing, but since I myself am a marketer I should not fall into the maya-jaal.' This was years before the entire Business class came down to pay homage to Sonia Gandhi when she began to fly Economy (or 'cattle class' according to Shashi Tharoor's infamous tweet) as part of the Congress's austerity drive in 2009."

MNC VS VC VS MD

Director-level appointees realize that first encounters with the VC are usually of the third kind.

The Times traditionally grew its own senior managers. Though Satish Mehta and Ram Lakshman had been lured away from the cigarette and hotel divisions of ITC respectively, most of the generals during Ashok Jain's chairmanship had risen from the trenches. PR Krishnamurthy, who became GM in the then omnipotent Bombay office, had started out as a humble personal secretary in Sahu Jain & Co before his formidable legal and accounting talents were discovered and developed.

The next generation saw it differently. They had to. The new-media ambitions demanded people with the tech-entertainment pizzaz and experience that nothing in the group's traditional business could provide. Pradeep Guha alone had the innate flash (surprising for a man who had started life as a leftist). The brothers began picking MNC cherries.

The MD looked out for those with professional expertise; the VC's transfusion efforts were prompted as much by his own need to draw on high 'IP', intellectual property.

Ravi Dhariwal and Mahendra Swarup were two head honchos from Pepsico Ltd assiduously headhunted at the turn of the millennium. The former had wanted to complete his Philippines posting, but Swarup, who had already returned to India, was able, available and raring.

MNC VS VC VS MD

He was inducted to bring his global marketing skills to Vineet's baby, Times Internet Ltd. Before formally starting he naturally had to meet Samir Jain.

Mahendra Swarup had been struck by flu, but he went anyway at the appointed time to Jain House at 6, SP Marg, then still the whole family's address. If he had been less of a newbie, he would have postponed the meeting because Samir Jain is extremely susceptible to colds, and immediately dispenses with anyone with the slightest sniffle. (People have been known to fake coughs when they anticipate a difficult meeting with VC.)

People have been known to fake coughs when they anticipate a difficult meeting with VC.

However, Swarup recalled an extremely solicitous Samir Jain not dispensing with him, but dispensing medication. He summoned a minion to bring out an array of Ayurvedic pills and potions, and discussed their various powers. And that was the sum total of the 40-minute 'interview'. Later in the day, he even sent more vials to Swarup's house in Vasant Vihar.

The new head of TIL was then taken to 4, Tilak Marg to meet the Joint Managing Director, Nandita Jain, who lived there. Here too, it was all leisurely and personal, with no talk of his duties and responsibilities. The MNC man was taken aback at this unorthodox process of induction. His subsequent meeting with the MD, however, was "quick and business-like, to the point of being almost brusque".

From that very first meeting Swarup decided that "I would work for the Jains rather than for Bennett." It could not be otherwise because he grasped right then that the family was paramount. "I never met a single professional manager during my appointment and induction. Other family businesses put up a façade of professional management. The Jains don't bother. If they like you, you are on. It didn't matter a bit that I had no media experience at all."

It was no different for Ravi Dhariwal. He had come from Manila on a holiday, and decided he would pay a courtesy call to his potential employers. By this time, both Samir and Vineet Jain had moved into their separate wings of the grandly refurbished Sujagi on 15, Motilal Nehru Road. Dhariwal had been invited to meet them for breakfast, but found himself continuing on to lunch and then high tea, after which he was dropped to The Oberoi where he was staying.

He recalled that "VC kept plying me with food. It wasn't just about being correctly hospitable, but a much more personal involvement. It was exactly like our ancestral home in Rajasthan where my father would solicitously feed his guests. Having spent so much of my recent life abroad, I realized how self-conscious we had become about what was so natural in our traditions."

As with his erstwhile Pepsi colleague, Dhariwal's other enduring recollection of that first meeting was that "VC didn't speak at all about what he expected of me. Instead he chatted about my career, family, my pet hates and what I liked. He sat continuously throughout, while MD came and went from the room, and left for the office by lunch-time."

It didn't take him long to figure out that "The elder brother was unnervingly insightful and the younger was very matter of fact. It was The Sage vs The Achiever. Vineet said what he had to in two minutes, but Samir was on a long meditative journey. They complemented each other."

The November morning of 2001 when Dhariwal formally joined BCCL was equally non-MNC. "I was given this office. It was exactly as it is now, this same white board and these same rare Tanjore paintings. It used to be Nandita's room, so I felt privileged. But nobody came in to meet me, and I didn't know anyone I could go out and talk to. There was no VC, no MD in the office for the next six days."

MNC VS VC VS MD

The point is that none of his new colleagues helped him to settle. He just had to sort it out himself. There was no mentoring, you were your own navigator. It was all very congenial, but the subtext was clearly, 'Sure we'll be friends, but, look, this is my patch.'

The point is that none of his new colleagues helped him to settle. He just had to sort it out himself.

The non-MNC pattern continued. As soon as VC returned from Haridwar, he called Dhariwal not to his adjacent office, but to Sujagi. "We sat under a tree in the garden, and discussed a revision of the invitation price." This was the innovation which had changed the way papers were sold ever since VC decided to introduce it in TOI Delhi in 1992. The discussion rambled over various subjects and three days, "At Pepsi, it would have taken less than one hour. People came in, joined the discussion, and left."

Said Dhariwal, "Management training makes you think in a structured, linear way: this leads to this. The MD follows this thought pattern. VC, on the other hand, likes to ponder and mull over a decision, introduce apparently extraneous nuances. He brings several other disciplines into business thinking. The spirituality discipline rises above what is legally or professionally correct. Ethics is what we as mortals have decided as right and wrong. But the spiritual discipline is a code of consciousness."

For Swarup the early differentiator between the MNC and VC styles was the dining table. "Whenever we were at lunch, he observed what I relished in the lavish thali, and what I was ignoring. He told me what was good for me, and what I shouldn't eat. Not just that, he served me personally. And would often show up at my house followed by the driver staggering in with a large hot-case. He'd say, 'Mahendraji, aaj aap ki favourite kadhi banayi thi'."

Forget Jack Welch, can you imagine even Indra Nooyi arriving with an Igloo pack?

Dhariwal had had his grounding in companies such as Unilever where documentation was meticulous. And the financial choreography was adhered to. "In this family business, the style is more entrepreneurial. VC had such faith in the print business that crores were plunged into it without once having a discussion on ROI. In the same way, one never seriously hears of any market research or sees the kind of HR consultants who set up permanent residence in other companies." They do occasionally come and go, but mostly they go. It's a business run on instinct. And no one's complaining. Except those in other media houses who are then expected to reach the bar raised by BCCL.

An MNC is process-oriented, it swears by structure, and aims at creating the cookie-cutter manager. But here everyone is different, more surprising considering that all the strings are held in just two pairs of hands. Senior denizens of the rarefied floors will avow that there is never an attempt to 'Bennettise' a manager. Instead, his success is perceived in terms of how well he is 'aligned to the thinking of the Jains'.

Some may dismiss this as a distinction without a difference, but all the recent top dogs, Pradeep Guha, Arun Arora, AP Parigi, Vijay Jindal, Ravi Dhariwal, Rahul Kansal, the former adman who has shaped BCCL's distinctive caring brand, are indeed very different from one another.

This is a company quite unique. Everywhere else there is an agenda, you discuss the due matters, and then get on with the rest of your job. Here the darbar school of leadership prevails. It's an open house, the VC launches into a freewheeling monologue, and his'courtiers' challenge him with contrarian views, which VC loves, but takes only from select people. Someone presents a creatively crafted business phrase or a neologism, like an elegant couplet or complex aphorism in Emperor Akbar's diwan-e-khaas.

MNC VS VC VS MD

Food arrives for everyone. More people are summoned to partake of the philosophy being imparted and to add their lateral thought to the intellectual cauldron palpably bubbling. To the uninitiated it seems almost weird, but this is manthan Bennett style, and the resulting elixir is there for all to see, envy, perchance to emulate.

Here the darbar school of leadership prevails. It's an open house, the VC launches into a freewheeling monologue, and his 'courtiers' challenge him with contrarian views, which VC loves, but takes only from select people.

You never see people gathered in MD's office or his part of Sujagi immersed in a freewheeling discussion on any and every thing.

With the freedom of hindsight, Guha said, "If you were close to the maliks in a positive way, Times was an enriching experience. Otherwise it all depended on which boss you were blessed with or stuck with. Yes, there was an element of whim, and yes, this passed down to other bosses." VC is a huge admirer and encourager of the maverick. He's the biggest one of all.

This VC-MD JV is truly no MNC. It is a family house – and a surreal planet too. A story about Chairman's proposed nomination to the Rajya Sabha illustrates this. VC called a 'cabinet-level' meeting of his 'colleagues' and said that though there was an overwhelming view that she should be nominated, he believed otherwise. Why? Because she should not be in the same category as the MPs whom the TOI makes or breaks on any given day. The Chairman of BCCL should be above that common fray.

He then made a uniquely VC observation: “When any speaker comes up to the podium, he or she adjusts the mikes to the appropriate angle. Even the Prime Minister does it himself. But when Chairman steps up to the podium, someone else will always spring up to perform this mundane task for her.”

Having established such a long positioning lead, Bennett competes only with itself, with the brothers constantly shifting the goal posts; one physically, the other metaphysically. Swarup drew his analogy from another field. He called it “crucible management – VC and MD put in the salts, turn up the heat, and produce something new. This is also how they catalyse their managers. Use their strengths to align them with the business, their weakness as a goad to perform better.”

MD is concerned only with delivery. He is focused, result oriented, and impatient if tasks drag on. He keeps his cool (even his smile) right through, but it’s very clear that he’s unhappy and why.

Managers have often found themselves wondering how the two brothers can be so dissimilar, and the insightful have reached the conclusion that it is all a deliberate strategy. But, as always, the opposite also holds true. And that too is part of the rule by uncertainty.

Their passions are also different. Samir Jain continues to see print as the core. Vineet is the messiah of new media.

Vineet is not averse to celebrating the milestones of his new media empire in his trendy pad at Sujagi, opening bottles of champagne and wine, a concept alien to the Jains. He went to Swiss finishing school, remember? And, diametrically unlike his elder brother, he has a social life outside the Times. Exclusively so.

VC is the ascetic, spending long weeks at Haridwar, meditating over a strategy drawn from ancient wisdom but corporate enough to ulcerate his wanna-becomes.

At the same time, the avowed contrarian takes an impish delight in gossip.

Yes, Parivar Inc is more the former than the latter. Mahendra Swarup was as conscious of 'family' the day he left as on the day he joined. Ravi Dhariwal underlined how nothing pains both brothers more, and Samir more so, than a favourite employee leaving. It has nothing to do with what difference the departure will make to the bottom-line. It's something up close and personal. The leaver feels like a worm. And usually returns to the family, and I mean family, sooner or later, as I can vouch for from a thirty-year relationship in three parts. Swarup got it right in a much shorter spell; 'You don't work for Bennett, you work for the Jains'. And only those who have worked with them in some degree of proximity will understand the complexity, and the simplicity, of this statement.

MNC VS VC VS MD

VC is the ascetic,
spending long weeks at Haridwar,
meditating over a strategy
drawn from ancient wisdom
but corporate enough
to ulcerate his wanna-becomes.

***

Every mythology needs a central core. And every mythology also needs a maverick. Sometimes both can be the same.